HOW TO WRITE
AND SELL INTERVIEWS

HOW TO WRITE AND SELL INTERVIEWS

Sally-Jayne Wright

a&b

First published in Great Britain in 1995 by
Allison & Busby
an imprint of Wilson & Day Ltd
179 King's Cross Road
London WC1X 9BZ

A catalogue record for this book is available from
the British Library.

ISBN 0 74900 207 7

Designed and typeset by N-J Design Associates
Romsey, Hampshire
Printed and bound in Great Britain by
Redwood Books, Trowbridge, Wiltshire

To Ginge

Thanks to William Cook, Lesley Dobson, Barbara Ewing, Gillian Fairchild, Duncan Fallowell, Gary Jenkins, Ann Lloyd, Dee Remmington, Val Sampson, Joyce Walter and everybody else I interviewed about interviewing.

CONTENTS

1. OPPORTUNITY KNOCKS   1
You, too, can interview famous people.
The skills every writer needs.
The types of interview.
Anecdotes and quotations.
Whom to talk to.
What to write about.
Selling for beginners.

2. LET'S GET STARTED   12
How to study markets.
The topical hook.
The timely hook.
How to sell your ideas to editors.
Testing your ideas.
Your clippings files.
Spot the professional.

3 HUMAN INTEREST FEATURES   21
What is a human interest feature?
The market.
Where to find ideas.
Persuading your subjects to talk.
Selling your idea to the editor.
The interview.
Getting the style right
Where beginners go wrong – editors speak out.

4. CELEBRITY INTERVIEWS   35
What is a celebrity?
Realistic goals.
The publicity machine.
Good beginners' markets.
Round-ups.
How to track down famous people.
How to sell celebrity interviews.
Developing a speciality.

5. PREPARING FOR THE INTERVIEW 46
How to find experts.
Researching celebrities.
Taking notes.
Interviewing by telephone.
Ten tips on telephone technique.
Fixing the time/place/day.
Your interview survival kit.

6. QUESTION TIME 56
How to prepare your questions.
Essential questions.
How to write open-ended questions.
The wrong questions.
Questions that get results.
Top tips from professionals.
Sell your interview again.
Checking your questions.

7. THE BIG DAY 70
Opening the interview.
Body language.
Interview etiquette.
What to wear.
Getting the best out of the interviewee.
Don't forget the details.
Controlling the interview.
Closing the interview.

8. TRICKY INTERVIEW SITUATIONS 82
Typical problems and their solutions (question and
answer session).
Can I see your copy? (No).
Can I see your copy? (Yes).
Off the record/on the record.
Better safe than sorry.

9. WRITING UP THE INTERVIEW 94
Transcribing your tape.
The different interview formats.

Tips on writing the profile.
Openings with impact.
Endings that satisfy.
Polish, polish, polish.

10. ANY OTHER BUSINESS? 104

10. ANY OTHER BUSINESS?   104

The selling power of pictures.
What rights have you sold?
Money, money, money.
Getting down to work.
Your support network.
Growing your career.

APPENDIX

Fig 1 Example of a query letter   111
Fig 2 Sample cover page   112
Fig 3 How to lay out the first page of your article   113
Fig 4 The written approach   114

INDEX 115

INDEX   115

1

OPPORTUNITY KNOCKS

You, too, can interview famous people

Behind every famous person interviewed in a Sunday paper or glossy magazine, there's someone else asking the questions. Why shouldn't that someone be you?

What could be more enjoyable than meeting new people, asking them interesting questions, writing it up, seeing your name in print and getting paid for it? Especially if, at the same time, you've had a chance to read their new book, indulge your taste for tennis or get free tickets for their new show?

You don't have to be famous to do it. You don't even have to have worked on a newspaper and magazine to break in. (Though I'm not saying contacts don't help.)

This book is for the writer with little experience but big ambitions. It will help not just the would-be celebrity interviewer but anyone wishing to write non-fiction articles for magazines and newspapers. The same basic principles apply. If you have sold one or two articles but would like to try celebrity interviews and human interest features, it will help you too. With application, some insider tips and a real understanding of how to aim at a market, there's no reason why you should not sell your work.

While you'll discover how to track down and interview famous people, you'll also acquire professional skills used by journalists to interview the person in the street. You'll learn how to forage for facts, encourage opinions and solicit sensitive stories.

Many writers find so-called *ordinary* people more fascinating than the famous and earn good livings as writers of human interest features. In Chapter 3, we look at how to write and sell the increasingly popular real life and triumph-over-tragedy stories.

I once asked such a writer what motivates her to make a living this way. "I'm insatiably nosy," came the reply. "And one day I'd like to write fiction." Where better to research characters, plots, motives, background and dialogue than talking to the wide variety of people you'll meet on your interviews? It's excellent background whatever writing ambitions you have.

You can't live every sort of lifestyle but in interviewing others about theirs, on their own territory, you'll gain insight into many different worlds and professions. As a freelance writer, I've spoken to people as varied as the manager of a sausage factory, a Turkish nomad, an actress in her dressing-room and a commercial diver out at sea.

To learn to interview is to learn to listen. And as you become a better listener, you will acquire the art of bringing people out. You will talk to experts, professionals and enthusiasts. It is very rewarding to talk to someone on a subject he feels passionate about, feel him warm to the subject and proudly show off his expertise. Both the enthusiasm and the knowledge will rub off on you.

As you grow in your career, you can develop your writing in line with your own interests. If you love clothes, why not specialise in talking to fashion designers about their creations? Love jazz? Become the expert on jazz musicians.

While satisfying my curiosity and indulging my interests, writing and selling interviews also combines my two favourite hobbies. Writing – and meeting new people. Wouldn't you like to make money in such a way? Read on.

The skills every writer needs

To write and sell interviews successfully requires a wide range of skills. And that's before the writing even begins. In the first place, you'll need to be a good salesperson. Whether on the phone, in person, or in a letter, you'll need to persuade the interviewee to talk to you. You'll need good telephone manners, the ability to gain trust quickly, present yourself in a credible manner and to establish a rapport.

In the course of your work you'll speak to people from all walks of life. Like the shrewd salesperson, you'll use your intuition to "read" people and decide how best to appeal to them. Perhaps you can flatter the expert to share some of his knowledge with you. Or could you use your genuinely sympathetic personality to persuade an upset mother to tell you her sad story?

Like the efficient salesperson, you'll be persistent in a subtle way. You'll need staying power if you're going to "chase" a celebrity or her agent to give you an interview. Persistence pays off, too, when gathering material. When talking to several people for a feature, I invariably find that the very last person I talk to gives me the most interesting story.

What about the interview itself? A genuine interest in, even nosiness about, other people is essential. If you aren't interested in what a person is saying, it shows. The sensitive salesperson does not stick to a script. He varies his pitch according to the personality of the other person, changes tack if he sees one line of questioning is more fruitful than another. Yes, you'll need the ability to think on your feet – and it can be hair-raising at times.

Finally, and more important than anything else I've written here, you'll need the ability to LISTEN. That's why quiet, shy people can make excellent interviewers. In fact, if you're the outgoing, "life-and-soul-of-the-party" type, you may need to suppress your talkative side, at least during interviews.

The good news is that the more interviewing you do, the better you get. Interviewing and listening skills will help not just in your writing but in many other areas of your life. For example, at a social or business function, interviewing techniques can make you much more successful at getting to know a roomful of new faces. Instead of talking about yourself, you'll find out about them. In any situation where negotiation is involved, interviewing skills can give you the upper hand. I believe that in any dialogue, it's the person who does more listening, not talking, who holds more power.

Many people find their newly acquired listening skills make them more confident with strangers at parties and with the opposite sex. Ask a new person about herself, take a real interest and you'll soon lose your shyness. What's your definition of charm? Is it the person who talks about himself all evening or the person who shows a genuine interest in you?

The types of interview

To get your imagination going, let's look at the types of interview you could sell. First, let's consider the *profile* – a short biographical or character sketch – usually of a famous person. This is the category you associate with interviews. It may involve talking to Anthony Hopkins only or, in an in-depth interview, quizzing his family, friends and colleagues.

Not everyone wants to write about the famous. You could pen a profile on an ordinary person provided he is, in some way, extraordinary. In *Bella*, I read an amusing feature about a vicar who tap-dances and abseils from the church roof. One opportunity to interview ordinary folk is if the profile fits into a regular "slot". Such a feature appears each week in a magazine and always has the same theme and number of words. For example, in a slot called "Ideal for Working Mums" in *Best*, I read an interview with a lollipop lady. Though working, she can still meet her children from school. Keep scouring magazines and newspapers for these regular slots and you'll soon generate plenty of ideas. (Ordinary people who have battled over extraordinary circumstances are a separate category. So-called triumph-over-tragedy features will be covered in Chapter 3.)

Many features involve interviewing more than one person. In the *round-up*, as the name suggests, a selection of opinions is rounded up for your article. The reader gets the impression that the people are all gathered together in a room to discuss a particular subject. For example, in a frivolous piece which appeared in the *Daily Telegraph*, well-known people offered their comments on the new longer skirt lengths; in *Femail* magazine, five women talked about what it's like to work nude as an artist's model.

The people rounded up don't have to be well known. A freelance journalist writing for the *Guardian* every week asked the residents of particular towns to comment on a topical issue. Pensioners, pub owners and mechanics all chipped in. To make the idea more entertaining, each week, the journalist linked the topic with the name of the town. She asked, "What do the people of Manley think of male au-pairs?"

"Children under 12 should be banished from cafés and diners," says an interviewee in *Best*. The slot is called Matter of Opinion. Yet another category you could consider is the *debate*. Your topical theme could be anything, serious or not, provided the people you interview have differing views.

Popular with monthly magazines is the *composite* feature. Three interviewees (sometimes more) relate their experiences, good and bad, on a given subject. It might be anything from what it's like to be adopted, to what it's like to buy a home in Spain. The *case histories* follow an introduction by the writer and an expert comment. Perhaps you could interview three people who live aboard houseboats or find five sets of sisters and ask them how they get along?

Anecdotes and quotations

One definition of an interview is a "conversation held between two people in order to obtain information". It is from such exchanges together with research that you will gain the raw material to write your articles and features.

But why talk to anybody at all? Why not simply research your subject in the local library, write it up and sell it?

The simple answer is that you could do but the result would not be true journalism. An article put together from research is known by journalists as "cut and paste". But journalism is "the collecting and presenting of facts and opinions about *current* events and topics of *public interest*". You couldn't find out what Joe Bloggs thinks on a current issue *today* by looking it up in the library. Even if such information were recorded, it would already be out of date. There's another reason to talk to people. Interviewees provide you with anecdotes or examples. In a light-hearted article on the hobby, juggling, I wrote:

> Mark from Norfolk reckons keeping his eye on the ball
> has cleared up his latent stomach ulcer. Before he started
> juggling regularly, the only way to control the pain was a
> strong pain-killer administered by his doctor.

The story of Mark from Norfolk is an anecdote or example. It is much more interesting that if I had merely said, "Juggling has some surprising health benefits".

Anecdotes provide the storyteller's touch and lighten your writing. In one paragraph, sometimes more, you'll tell a little story that illustrates the point you are making. As you speak to people, you should constantly be asking them, "Can you give me any examples?"

The more visual your examples, the better. In the following anecdote, from the same article, the reader gets a vivid picture.

> Juggling balls are filled with birdseed. Liz, a systems ana-
> lyst, has already discovered this. Her Dad accidentally
> threw one onto the log fire at Christmas.

Anecdotes often take the form of quotations. Quotations are another way to move your writing along. It is proven that readers are more likely to read anything which appears within speech marks.

> "Juggling relaxes your body and mind," says Jan, a com-
> puter systems analyst. "It has no side effects, unlike
> smoking and alcohol. It's also good for showing off at
> parties."

Remember, we said a good interviewer has to be persistent? You may have to talk to dozens of people to acquire the anecdotes and quotations you will use in your finished article. To obtain the examples above, I spoke to countless people on the spot, under stressful circumstances, ducking and dodging the flying balls. I was about to give up when I landed on a woman with red hair and an earring in her nose.

"I'm getting married in June and I want fire-eaters and jugglers at my wedding. My boyfriend is going to ride his unicycle and we want all the guests to learn to juggle."

This sounded so off-beat and fun that, of course, it was the anecdote I used to end my piece. The anecdote contained a quotation.

Whom to talk to

To gather your anecdotes and get your information, you will talk to three categories of people: experts, the person-in-the-street and famous people.

In the first category are *experts* to lend your writing weight and authority. Experts give informed opinions. Mrs Bloggs next door could tell me all about the health benefits of beetroot but I doubt whether I'd use her opinions in my feature. The reason is she's neither a doctor, a nutritionist, a professional beet-grower nor any other kind of expert.

An expert is the official spokesman on a subject. "Would you use the Channel Tunnel?" asked the writer of a feature which appeared in *Bella*. In the course of the piece, she spoke to representatives from Eurotunnel, the Fire Brigades Union, the British Safety Council and the Channel Tunnel Safety Authority. She even asked a clinical psychologist for an opinion on claustrophobia. Would you have been interested in the article if she had spoken only to Mr Smith, his son and the local taxi driver? The man or woman in the street, on the other hand, represents a typical point of view. Perhaps you're writing a piece on whether parents should smack their children. You'd talk to parents with both points of view.

You will notice that most articles combine material gathered from both sources: the person in the street and experts. In an article I wrote on smoke-free restaurants, pubs and other places to meet in London, I spoke to smokers and non-smokers. For an official opinion, I contacted, among others, A.S.H. (Action on Smoking and Health), a pub owner and the press officers of

McDonald's and Debenhams, two chains which have no-smoking areas.

The numerous "relationships" features which appear in women's magazines are also a good example of this combination. Let's say three ordinary women relate their personal experiences of marital infidelity. For weight and authority, the writer also seeks the official view of a psychologist and a marriage guidance counsellor.

If, on the other hand, you decide you would like to write and sell human interest interviews (see Chapter 3), you will talk exclusively to the ordinary person who has had some extraordinary experience. The fact that she is, indeed, "someone just like me" gives this kind of interview added reader appeal.

In the third category of interviewees are famous people. It could be anyone in the public eye from a politician to a pop star. With the public appetite for celebrities being what it is, almost anything this person has to say is of interest. (See Chapter 4 for celebrity interviewing.) You may be talking to a famous person in depth for a profile or getting a brief opinion which you'll combine with others, such as, "Your favourite beauty tip".

The famous person can also serve the function of expert. In an article on fitness, you might ask a football star how he keeps in shape. Faced with two expert opinions, it's the well-known expert who gives your article more force.

What to write about

To a writer, ideas are income. A freelance writer won't survive unless he can keep coming up with ideas. The amateur crumbles when his one inspiration is rejected; the professional has plenty more. Do you have what it takes? Panic not, there are ideas everywhere if you know where to look.

If you have never been published, your first priority is to get into print. Seeing your by-line (your name under an article), and being paid for your work, will give you the injection of confidence every beginner needs.

So what could you write about? You could start close to home, with the obvious: your family, your friends, your job, your holiday, your hobbies. Let's say your friend is married to a professional bodybuilder. All weekend, she's been complaining what murder he is to live with in the weeks before a championship. Could you interview her about this for a women's magazine? I read such an article in *Ms London* and very funny it was, too.

Over the garden fence, your neighbour is assembling a kit car. Could you talk to him and write it up for a motoring magazine or the leisure section of a Sunday newspaper? In your local newspaper, there's a headline "Toddler injured as bus brakes". The toddler's teeth were smashed as he flew across the bus. Interview the parent and a representative of the bus company and you have the makings of a debate. "Should our buses have seat belts?"

To find ideas, you need to be alert and curious. Eavesdrop on conversations at the office, at the supermarket, in the bus queue. A friend phones you to say her boyfriend has dumped her without a word after a romantic skiing holiday. This has happened to another friend of yours. Is this the start of a relationships piece for a women's monthly?

One of the best sources of ideas are other people's features. Read, too, the classified advertisements in a publication, the readers' letters and the agony columns. "It's heartbreaking to hear of so many of today's generation being in debt," wrote a reader to *Women's Realm*. Could you write a piece on debt and divorce?

"Write about what you know," says every book on writing. I'd add,"Write what takes your fancy". Enthusiasm is infectious. If a subject fascinates you, you'll relish the research, the writing will be good and you'll entertain your reader.

Selling for beginners

"Could you go and interview Michael Jackson tomorrow, please?"

If only. As a freelance and a beginner, it will be up to you to sell your work to magazines and newspapers. The good news is that the potential market for your work is enormous. In 1993, 7000 periodicals were published in Britain. Of these, over 2000 were aimed at consumers and 5000 at the business community. You need only take a trip to the newsagents to see the countless titles on display: everything from *050* (for the over-fifties) to *Just Seventeen*. Both the women's and the leisure sections are impressive. Noticed how fat some of the Sunday newspapers are getting? Skim through all the various sections and think of all those pages to be filled every weekend. Why shouldn't some of those features be yours?

Countless magazines are printed which never appear at the newsagents. Think of all the free magazines available on the street – some eminent journalists have made their reputations here. There are company magazines, inflight magazines and magazines on subscription only. As an English speaker, you are fortunate – you can also sell your work in numerous countries that publish in English such as Australia, South Africa, the U.S.A. and the Far East.

To discover even more markets, check *The Writers' and Artists' Year Book* or *The Writer's Handbook*. A typical entry in the magazine section of the latter reads:

LOOKS
20 Orange Street, London, WC2H 7ED
Tel 0171 957 8383 Fax 0171 957 8400
Owner EMAP Women's Group Magazines
Editor Annabel Goldstaub
Circulation 231,000

Monthly magazine for young women aged 15-22, with emphasis on fashion, beauty and hair, as well as general interest features, including celebrity news and interviews, quizzes, etc. Freelance writers are occasionally used in all areas of the magazine. Contact the editor with ideas. Payment varies.

Wouldn't it be great to see your by-line in a glossy monthly or national newspaper? Don't lose sight of the dream, but concentrate first on getting into print. In choosing likely beginners' markets, concentrate on

maximising opportunity
minimising competition

It is logical that weeklies offer more opportunities than monthlies. They appear 52 times a year as opposed to only 12. The more
esoteric, smaller circulation papers will attract fewer competitors
than the nationals. Don't forget your regional papers.

Now the bad news. Though the field is wide open, the competition has never been so fierce. As well as their 6000 strong
membership, the National Union of Journalists estimates there are
another 3000 occasional and self-employed freelances in Britain.
In recent years, many magazines have merged and forced their
staff writers to go freelance. The editor will ring these tried and
trusted people first if there's an assignment going. Yes, you can
break in. But you'll need to study the publications you're aiming
at very carefully.

2

LET'S GET STARTED

OK, now you know what you want to write about, the other part of the equation is: what do the buyers of magazines and news-papers want to read about? You will be more successful if you direct your efforts according to sound marketing principles. Ask yourself: "What need do the readers have which I could fill? What are they interested in? What product (article) could I create to meet that need?"

Let's say the reader is a young, fashionable city dweller. Such people often live in cramped flats but desire a chic abode. A friend of yours is a designer. With clever use of a platform bed, mirrors and decor, he has made his studio flat appear twice the size. Interview him, explain how it's done and you've fulfilled a reader need.

How to study markets

Professionals don't talk about magazines or papers, but markets where they can sell their work. To find suitable markets for your words, start with the publications you already read. If you've been digesting the *Daily Mail* over your branflakes every morning since the year dot, you are the typical reader. If an idea excites you, it will interest most of your fellow readers. This applies to your specialist publication or trade paper and the leisure magazine to which you have a subscription. These are your primary markets. Set yourself a target of three for close study. You need to buy at least six recent issues.

12

Read, read, read. Would-be celebrity interviewers should be scouring the women's, TV and showbiz-related magazines and appropriate pages of the dailies (more in Chapter 4); for human interest features, try the women's weeklies and tabloid newspapers. Please don't be mean about buying magazines. Periodicals and papers bought by freelance writers are tax-deductible. A freelance journalist interviewed on the radio claimed he could sell £1500 worth of work from a £15 investment at W.H. Smith.

Now that you've got your hands on the goods, your first step is to figure out how much of the magazine, if any, is written by freelances. Look to the front (or sometimes the back) of the magazine to what is known as the masthead. Here you'll find the names of the editor, features editor and so on, right down to advertising sales and subscriptions. If the names under the features match up with those on the masthead, too bad. If, however, there are several contributors not listed on the masthead, this could be your lucky day.

What do the advertisements show? Advertisers aren't daft. They wouldn't pay all that money to advertise unless guaranteed a certain target reader. In the free magazine, *Ms London* (available on the street), the pages abound with advertisements for sunbeds, contact lenses, a girls' night out at a popular nightspot, cheap flights and cheap hairdos. The classifieds seek secretaries of 21–30. Conclusion: reader is a fun-loving, 21–30-year-old working woman, adventurous and interested in saving money.

At the other end of the spectrum, *Choice*, Britain's magazine for successful retirement, features advertisements for legacies, bath and stair lifts, retirement homes. This reader is financially secure as the advertisements for exotic holidays and new cars confirm.

The topical hook

With every idea you suggest, you should ask yourself, "What's new about this? What's topical about this? Why should the editor take my idea NOW?"

The finer you can tune your idea to a *topical hook*, the better, especially for newspapers. I once spoke to executives who were learning to juggle to relieve stress. It sold to the *Independent*. In making the idea more relevant, I asked myself, "What are the readers (predominantly male professionals) particularly stressed about NOW?" This formed the topical hook which appeared in the first sentence:

> If all this worry about losing your job is getting to you, there's a remedy. Learn to juggle.

Most news-oriented of the main print media are evening papers which can run a leader on a story which happened only this morning. They are followed by dailies, weeklies, then monthlies and quarterlies. The topical link is always apparent. A Hollywood star has a new fitness video out, so profiles appear in all the leading magazines. A famous politician cheats on his wife sparking endless features on marital infidelity. There's a new bill to force Rottweiler owners to muzzle their pets, so you read several debates on the issue.

The timely hook

If your topical hook is very obvious – perhaps your idea links in with a new, well-hyped film – staff writers will invariably beat you to it. It may be more profitable for the freelance writer to be timely, rather than topical.

Editors are always looking for a fresh slant on Christmas, the January sales, Mother's Day and so on. Could you talk to the man who writes Christmas cracker jokes or ask seven fashion experts to name the ultimate scoop in the January sales? An unusual slant for Mother's Day would be to interview three people who were dropped on doorsteps as babies and don't know their real mother. This idea appeared in the *Sunday Times*.

Of course, your competitors will also be sending in timely ideas. Why not research a more unusual anniversary, for example, X years ago today, the bikini was "invented". Look this up using a dictionary of dates in your local library. Use one such as the *Encyclopedia of Dates and Events*, (Headway 1991).

Now get organised. If your ideas are going to be linked to a date, get your calendar out and start planning. You need to submit your ideas well in advance. Monthly magazines work four to six months ahead, weeklies ten to twelve weeks, and dailies two weeks to a month. July is <u>not</u> too early to submit an idea for Christmas. Remember you will not only need enough time to prepare your letter of enquiry. You also need time to send it to another publication if the first editor turns you down. One advantage of a timely idea is that it obliges the editor to make a quick decision.

How to sell your ideas to editors

As a writer, you are a salesman in a buyer's market and the buyers are magazine and newspaper editors. How do you get your wares in front of them? A letter of enquiry known as a *query letter*, mailed or faxed, is the best approach.

One reason to write, rather than phone, is that the editor, with 1001 other things on her mind, may be too harassed to give your idea due attention. It's easier to say no than yes when under pressure. Your query letter:

● Sets out what your idea is, clearly and succinctly, in the first couple of sentences. (Not only will the idea dazzle them, so will the quality of your writing.)

● Tells the editor how you mean to proceed and what ground you'll cover

● Tells the editor why you're the ideal person to write this piece

There are as many styles of query letter as there are writers. Appendix Fig 1 shows you one approach. The first thing you'll notice is that I've addressed the letter to an individual rather than vaguely, "the editor". If you don't know the person responsible for a section give the paper a ring and ask.

Editors are busy people, so your letter has about four seconds to make an impression. Don't open apologetically with "I am a journalist and I wondered if . . ." Get to the point. In the sample on page 111, I decided to put the topical hook right at the beginning.

Good query letters leave the editor panting to discover more. In the sample, I've given, for example, tell her there's a Cardiff GP who prescribes juggling for stress. But don't reveal where he lives and his phone number. You'll tell all when you write the finished article. Next, after outlining how you mean to proceed, make it clear you are professional and that the article is *for sale*. Many books on writing suggest you attach a stamped addressed envelope. Personally, I believe you should not be so humble. Editors would be out of a job without good, original ideas and talented people like you to write them. I also think an SAE looks amateur and invites refusal.

A good rule of selling is "make it easy for the customer to buy". If you haven't worked for the magazine before, tell the editor you will be happy on write the article "on spec" (on a speculative basis). That means you'll have to write the whole feature and the magazine will decide whether to publish.

If after ten days to two weeks, you haven't heard anything, follow up your letter with a polite phone call. "Did you get my idea on x?" The editor's assistant will often be able to help you. However good your idea, the decision to take it will be subjective. An editor who smokes 60 a day may not fancy a feature on celebrities who gave up smoking. A year later, when she has turned her back on tobacco, you may be more fortunate.

Testing your ideas

Now you're in the editor's chair. What would you say to someone who rang you up and asked "Would you like something on Michael Aspel?" If you were busy and having a bad day, you might well say "No, thanks," and hang up. But probably, you'd ask the person to be more specific.

16

"What's your angle?"

Your ideas must be specific, or as journalists say, have an *angle*. An angle is a specific viewpoint or a look at one isolated aspect of a subject. What Michael Aspel watches on TV is an angle. Why Michael Aspel decided to buy a farm in Tuscany (he hasn't, to my knowledge!) is an angle. Be specific and always tell the editor what's new about the idea. Emphasise originality, new thoughts, new developments, new experiences, new findings.

Let's assume you suggest the piece on the farm in Tuscany. The editor's next thought is whether you are qualified to write the piece. Are you Michael Aspel's next-door neighbour in Tuscany? The estate agent who sold him the farm? A personal friend? Mention any relevant writing experience if you can but don't worry if you can't. It's the quality of the finished writing that counts in the end.

Before you send that letter out, check carefully what you've written. Ask yourself:

1. Have I checked that Sam Hack is still the editor and have I spelt his name correctly? (There's nothing worse than sending your carefully drafted letter to the wrong person.)

2. Has this idea been done before or is it genuinely new? (If the idea *has* been done before, is your slant sufficiently fresh and original?)

3. Have I given a reason why the editor should buy this feature NOW? (The topical hook.)

4. Does the main idea appear in the first paragraph?

5. Have I given a reason why I should write this article rather than someone else? (For example, if it is an article about schools, it is worth mentioning that you are a teacher.)

6. From my query letter, would I want to know more about the subject or do I know the whole story already?

7. Do I sound confident and enthusiastic, or negative and apologetic?

8. Is the query letter itself well written considering this is a sample of the goods to follow?

9. Have I fitted my idea on to one side of A4 paper? (If not, be more succinct.)

10. If I were the editor, would I stake my reputation and budget on this idea?

A well-written query letter serves as a script if you ever have to phone the editor. It helps to convince you (or not) that you're ready to write the article. If you somehow can't set the idea down in writing, perhaps it's not such a good idea after all. Finally, I shouldn't have to say this but ... never promise an idea that you're not in a position to write.

Your clippings files

Newspapers are precious materials to the beginner writer. It is from them that you'll build a mini-library stacked with relevant research – otherwise known as your clippings files.

Under clippings, I mean anything that might be useful: business cards, theatre programmes, advertising flyers. I store my cuttings in A4-sized used manila envelopes, marking the front of each envelope with the subject e.g. *celebrity round ups*. When one envelope becomes too full, sub-divide into smaller categories. You might use coloured envelopes, boxes or hanging files. The point is that you know where everything is and can retrieve it with the minimum of fuss.

As soon as you have sold your first feature on a subject, you will be ready to open your specialist files. For example, if you sell an interview with Joanna Lumley, thereafter anything else which appears on the actress should be clipped and filed. The next time you interview her, you'll dip into your file to prepare an update, being even better informed as to her career moves, views and hobbies.

Next, scour all magazines and papers for likely markets or slots. "I could write a feature like that," you say to yourself, as traffic warden, Tracey, describes her job to a women's weekly. Clip it out. If you're planning a serious attack on that section, clip out at least six examples, more if possible. These are your market files.

I'm particularly fond of my file simply called *ideas*. Here are weird and wonderful ideas for people I *could* interview: a woman arm-wrestler, a spokesman from the British tarantula collecting society, two men who started a cockroach extermination team under a Government business start-up scheme. You won't necessarily use any of your ideas. But when that rainy day arrives, work is slack, and you need to send out a whole lot of query letters, a troll through the file will get your creative juices flowing.

Spot the professional

Earlier, I estimated that you have, at a conservative guess, 9000 competitors. Nevertheless, editors are ever on the lookout for reliable new writers.

But it is unlikely an editor will commission work (give you a firm order) if she's never seen your writing. (Would you?) What she will do, if she likes your idea, is to ask you to send in the article on spec. If this happens, you should ask for a deadline, an exact word count (the number of words required) and discuss the specifics with the editor so that as far as possible you can fulfil her requirements.

Then you should write and send the article. This is your first professional test. Many new writers, terrified by a "yes", disappear into the night and are never heard of again. Editors have seen it all before. The professional submits the article on time, with the right number of words, with every word correctly spelt and no factual errors.

Another compulsory sign of the professional is a typed manuscript. If you have no keyboard skills, learn. Computers, word processors and printers are improving all the time. As more and more of your fellow writers acquire better equipment, so the quality of their presention is better too.

Anything handwritten is taboo. Don't assist your competitors by delivering grubby, slipshod work. Use clean, good quality paper (not flimsy "onion skin"). Send in your work double spaced, on one side of the paper only, with two-inch margins all round. Attach a cover page. Figs. 2 and 3 on pages 112 and 113 show you how you could set it out.

In the next two chapters, we'll be looking at two of the best paying interview markets: human interest features and celebrity interviews. But first, a word of caution. In your enthusiasm to see your name in print, you may be prepared to write for nothing. Work for a lower fee, by all means, but never give your services FREE. You're a professional writer only when someone's prepared to pay for your work. And on that professional note, let's move on.

3

HUMAN INTEREST FEATURES

Real life is more moving than any fiction. If you're inspired by the sheer courage of ordinary folk in adversity, you should be talking to them. When it comes to selling your interviews, one of the best paid markets – and the most fascinating – is the human interest feature.

What is a human interest feature?

Strictly speaking, any story about people, rather than issues, is a human interest feature. Your interview with the vicar who tap dances, or your feature about living with a bodybuilder contain human interest. But what journalists tend to mean when they talk about human interest features are stories of individuals who have triumphed over extraordinary circumstances – or misfortunes. So-called triumph-over-tragedy stories – TOTs for short – would fall into this category.

The skills described in this chapter will help you write not only human interest features but the *case history* type of interview described in Chapter 1. In both you'll be hearing the experiences of ordinary people. The difference is that in the case history, the interview is only part of your article; in human interest, it's the whole feature.

A good human interest story has all the elements of a good plot in a short story or novel. It involves a sympathetic hero who fights against overwhelming odds to resolve a conflict of some kind and finally wins through. The more twists and turns to the plot the better. Romeo and Juliet who fall in love against their parents' wishes and eventually commit suicide would count as a human interest feature.

The Americans call human interest features *true life dramas* and this name serves to remind us that a good story contains drama. The greater the conflict, the greater the story. A person about to be evicted from his home is dramatic, but a child saved from death by drowning more so.

As with the short stories you read in magazines, human interest features usually have a happy, or so-called "upbeat" ending. Even if the events of the story were tragic, the ending should inspire hope for the future. In writing human interest features, you should appeal to the emotions; the reader wants to be moved.

The heroes and heroines are normal people like you and me. It's important that the reader identifies with them and feels for them in their hour of need. The reader is left with the feeling: "There, but for the grace of God, go I". The highest paid feature in this category is the celebrity human interest feature. These are the stories about the actor who overcame his alcoholism, the TV fitness queen who survived breast cancer, the famous jockey who went to jail. The more "public" the person, the more saleable your piece will be. Unless a story falls in your lap, or someone trusts you a great deal, celebrity or royal human interest features are for later in your career.

The market

Once upon a time, human interest features were mainly to be found in newspapers, in the form of hard-hitting news stories. Then with the proliferation of women's weekly news magazines in the late-80s, the market exploded and the desire for the in-depth emotional story was born.

Step into your local newsagent today and you'll find human interest features across the board. In a Sunday supplement, a tennis champion is revealing how he discovered he had AIDS; in the

Real Life section of the *Sunday Mirror,* a woman reveals how she beat cancer and learned how to feel sexy again. The women's weeklies and TV magazines are crammed with such stories.

In a recent issue of *Bella* I discovered the following typical mix of stories:

- a couple who both suffer from epilepsy meet in hospital and marry against the odds.
- a young man's wife and five-month-old baby are killed by a hit and run driver. He finds happiness again with a second wife and family.
- a woman's beloved horse is sold to an unscrupulous dealer. She goes to court and wins him back.
- a woman thinks she's had a miscarriage but later discovers she is 15 weeks pregnant with the same baby.

The best markets for the beginner are, as usual, those publications which take the most, publishing not two, but ten stories every week. The best advice if you would like to write a human interest feature is to read them. Can't think what to write about? Start with the main events of human life: birth, love, death.

It's a proven fact known to advertisers that women are more likely to look at an advertisement featuring a baby. They also like reading about them. A good family story featuring a baby has a good chance of selling. For example, how a baby was kidnapped from the supermarket and won back.

If readers enjoy fictional romance, they're even more warmed to read of a true life love story. But to qualify for the human interest category, it must be true that "the course of true love never did run smooth". Obstacles in your love story could include:

- an age imbalance
- parental disapproval
- physical separation perhaps even by marriage to different partners
- disability or illness
- a love triangle

The ultimate human battle is the struggle against death. Could you write about the couple who decide to marry even though she has only one year left to live? The bravery of human beings faced with certain death, pain and suffering is impossible to believe, so write about it.

It's always helpful to return to fiction for ideas. Just as we are pleased to see David win out against the mighty Goliath, so the triumph of the individual against the system makes a good story. Many of the weeklies carry a *justice* story in which an individual fights back. You could write for example about:

- a woman who fends off a mugger
- a woman whose hair is ruined at the hairdresser. She sues for negligence and wins
- a woman who successfully sues a car dealer for selling her a deathtrap.

You could also write about the triumph of an individual against overwhelming odds. Example: a woman loses ten stone to marry her fiancé.

Early in your writing career, you will need to find which stories make you feel more comfortable. It takes a certain kind of person to want to talk to the wife of convicted murderer, or a person diagnosed with a terminal disease. Perhaps you have this talent. If not, and you prefer to leave those stories to more experienced writers, there are still ways to break in. Good markets for the beginner include success stories, love stories and personal heroics, for instance the story of a woman who walked across Antarctica. Read, read, read and the ideas will soon come.

Where to find ideas

Some time ago, I was walking along a street in Central London when I spotted a woman in her 50s wearing a sandwich board. Was she advertising a new service, or begging for cash? No, her simple hand-written message read: *Book-keeper, 30 years experi-*

ence, seeks work. Unable to find a job and encountering ageism wherever she turned, this proud woman had been forced to take drastic measures. It was a story. The book-keeper found a job and I sold the article to *Bella* – it appeared under their success story section.

One way to find ideas is to do as I did and follow your natural curiosity. I once saw the following advertisement on a postcard in my local newsagent's: *surrogate mother wanted to give couple a baby.* Follow your natural curiosity and see where it takes you. Don't ignore your immediate surroundings, either. Have any of your friends, relatives or acquaintances triumphed over extraordinary misfortune?

The obvious place to look for stories is in national newspapers. But remember the principle mentioned in Chapter 1 about making life easier for yourself? Your aim as a beginner is to cut down the competition. Staff journalists read the daily papers, so do seasoned freelances. As one editor told me, if a cracking story comes up, there may be anything from two to five publications chasing it: perhaps two women's weeklies, a TV magazine, a daily tabloid newspaper and one of the Sundays. Why should people on staff send you, the unknown, to chase a story when they have experienced freelances on their books?

A better source would be your local papers. Perhaps you read of a schoolgirl who has fished her younger brother out of a pond, or a woman who has won back her job after unfair dismissal. Since the majority of your competition is resident in the south east, you'll have an advantage if you live in a less populated area. Staff writers might get the big regional papers but are often too busy to read them. And don't forget, if you can interest a magazine in your story, they'll pay your expenses to travel to the interview. One freelance I know who lives in London but is originally from the south west asks relatives to keep a close eye on her local paper back home. Not only does she have less competition, the features she sells help to pay for weekends in her home town.

A much more fruitful way of generating ideas is the "what if" approach. What's it like to lose your first-born to cot death syndrome? Does a mother feel terribly guilty? How does she feel when pregnant with her second child? Has anyone ever lost more than one child in this way? By contacting an infant death syndrome support group, you could uncover your own stories. You could ask them to put you in touch with victims of cot death syndrome.

Journalists stuck for ideas often generate stories from so-called "smouldering issues". Let's say, 18 months ago, a tower block in Manchester collapsed out of the blue. Although the story is several months old, the public still remembers it and it'll take only a bit of reminding from you to fan the flames. Could you interview a family involved in the disaster? All you'd have to do is get talking to the appropriate victim support group or relief organisation.

Still stuck for inspiration? Read the back issues of the magazine or paper you're aiming for. And remember the classic plots of fiction: *Cinderella, Romeo and Juliet, King Lear*.

Persuading your subjects to talk

Now you have the idea for a potential human interest feature, your next step is to track down the interviewee and secure that person's willingness to be interviewed. Trust is everything. In very many cases, an interviewee will agree to talk to you not because he trusts you but because he trusts *a third party*.

Let's say, for example, you are phoning the Foundation for the Study of Infant Deaths for a possible story on cot death. (I'll cover where to find such support groups in Chapter 5.) When you phone, you will need to be not only courteous but to explain exactly what your intentions are. You'll indicate whom the article is for and make it clear that the reason for writing it is to help other women. Like the good salesperson, you will need to overcome objections.

Perhaps the subject matter involved is so delicate that the interviewee will want complete anonymity. In that case, you will have to promise to change every detail that could identify the person, even the location if necessary. (And you'll need to check with the magazine that this is all right.) Usually, what happens then is that the support group will contact a suitable person and ask her permission for you to ring directly.

Where you have found a story in your local paper, on the other hand, you have no alternative but old-fashioned detective work. Obvious though it may sound, a logical place to look up your quarry is in the telephone directory. Your job will be easier if the person has an unusual name or the address is given in the newspaper. If the nature of the interview is very delicate, a sympathetic letter followed up by a phone call might be your best approach.

After that it's up to you, your telephone manner, your sensitivity and powers of persuasion. Let's say you want to talk to the parents of a child dying of some rare disease. He's not going to live beyond the age of 14. Why should they talk to you? In fact, there are several reasons: the rarer the circumstances of the family, the lonelier they will be. Talking to you can be therapeutic.

When people die, we remember them with a memorial stone or plaque. It is human to want your child to be remembered. Appeal to the parents' desire not to let their son be forgotten. Remind them that the story will be an inspiration for other parents in a similar situation. The readers will find out that it is possible to suffer the loss of a loved one and survive the experience. You should have no trouble at all getting a story from someone who has a desire for revenge or justice, or someone who has a happy success or love story to tell.

At this stage, you are having your preliminary conversation to gain more information and check that the story really is worth writing. You will, of course, tell the person that you're planning to offer it to *Woman's Realm* or *Best*. Some people will agree to talk to you because they like the magazine, or not, as the case may be. But it's better to find out now rather than later when you've offered it to the editor. You should also find out whether the person and her family are prepared to be photographed and more about the background.

Finally, there's one golden rule you should never forget. If you can avoid it, never use the word *interview*. Not only is it a daunting word associated with job applications and police interrogation, it makes the occasion out to be much too serious. "Can I come and talk to you, please?" will do fine.

Selling your idea to the editor

So you've found yourself a moving story and the central character is prepared to talk. Be enthusiastic and positive but, please, don't rush into things. Before contacting a busy editor with the "greatest story that ever was", run a few simple tests on your idea.

The first question to ask yourself is does your human interest story have a beginning, middle and an end? A story which doesn't have an ending is not a story. Let's say you've found the following tale in a local paper. A prison officer has been bitten by an HIV-positive prisoner. He's due to marry this summer and both he and his future wife are waiting anxiously for the results of his AIDS test. That would make a moving story, you think. You could interview the bride-to-be and the family. But gripping as this story seems, the story is not resolved. It will take three months for the test results to come through. You won't know the ending till that time is up. Clip the story out and do more detective work in a month or so.

Another question to ask yourself should be "Is the story about the kind of person normally covered in the magazine?" Triumph-over-tragedy features for the women's weeklies, for example, are about ordinary people. They don't cover the rich and powerful or those with dangerous jobs. The prison officer puts himself at risk as part of his day-to-day job. The story about the couple waiting to wed would have been more suitable if an ordinary person had been bitten. The heroes should be people with whom the reader can identify. If your reader is, for example, 20-30, married with children, the closer the hero is to the reader the better. The story should also be set in this country.

Now think your story through and examine the elements. Is it the kind of story you can tell in two sentences or does it have twists and turns? When you tell other people about your story, does it make them curious? A feature about a little boy in hospital who recovers from leukaemia is pleasant but so-so. A little boy who, while recovering from leukaemia, designs a buggy to help other little children, is a story with a twist.

Before preparing your approach, have one last check that you have all the facts at your fingertips. Perhaps your story is about an ordinary housewife who takes a crooked second-hand car dealer to court. The editor would expect you to name which court, when and where.

Finally, has the magazine done a similar one to the one you're offering in the last six months or year? While you can't know everything they've got up their sleeves you'll look pretty silly if a story similar to yours is splashed across the current issue.

If you've satisfied yourself you've eliminated the obvious causes for rejection, set down your idea on paper. If you're not known, it's best to write to start with and send your letter to the commissioning editor or features editor of the magazine. If you haven't heard within a week, give them a ring. Whether you phone or write, present your story as positively and confidently as you can. You won't sell a bad story to an editor by being confident but you may waste a good story with your nervousness and poor presentation.

Has the editor still turned you down? Don't worry. Magazines, like everything else, have their fashions in stories. Some editors are more receptive than others. Even seasoned freelances get their share of rejections. Keep the ideas coming in and sooner or later, you'll hit the jackpot.

The interview

What do you care more about, getting a good story at any price or the welfare of the person you're talking to? If you choose to specialise in human interest interviews, this is one decision you'll face early in your career.

A colleague of mine travelled several hours to do a major human interest interview for a national newspaper. She had taken great trouble to set up the interview through a third party, in this case a psychiatric social worker. But when she arrived, the mother and son of the family decided they didn't want to be interviewed after all. What did my friend do? Did she rant and rave? No, what she did was say: "I don't think it's right that we should try to coerce you. If you want me to go, I'll go and we'll forget the whole thing. Or I'll just go and have a walk around the block and give you time to talk about it. But if you really don't want to do it, we won't do it."

In the event, this saved the day. Because my friend was willing to give up the interview, the family trusted her. As my friend pointed out: "It's an article for me. It's a much bigger deal for them. It's their lives." If you're going to have any success at all, learn to be persistent but in a gentle way.

The commonest mistake for the newcomer is to try to rush a human interest interview. Usually, when setting up an interview, I let a person know how long I'm going to need him and try to stick to it (see Chapter 7). But in human interest interviewing, you need to allow as much time as it takes. Two to three hours possibly. Don't be too concerned to stick to your list of questions. The person knows why you have come to see him and what you're going to ask him. Let him find his own way of getting to the story and don't push too hard. You can prompt now and then only if he needs it.

It helps if you can empathise with the situation and get a good relationship going. You're interviewing the mother of a teenage son who has gone astray? Say, "That must be very worrying for you. I know, my sister-in-law has a teenage son and she has exactly the same problems."

A common mistake is to rush in and fill every silence. People need time to gather their thoughts and collect themselves. Never allow the following situation:

> Interviewer: And when did you first learn your son had multiple sclerosis?
> Interviewee: I was just going to tell you if you'd give me a chance.

While you should not be abrupt, don't be coy either. Difficult, searching questions will have to be asked and if you don't get around to it on the day of the interview, you'll only have to come back again. All the while that you are listening, you will be absorbing information. While not appearing to look down at your script, nevertheless, you must not be so absorbed that you forget to ask important details.

One advantage you have is that you're a stranger and, as everyone knows, it's much easier to tell a stranger about an intimate detail of your life. It's therapeutic to talk it out. In a short time, in a human interest interview you will build up an intense relationship: in fact, such a rapport that the interviewee will feel some emotional involvement with you. This is what psychologists call *transference*. After such a close encounter, you may even expect Christmas cards, regular phone calls and invitations to come and stay. This is an occupational hazard and if you can't handle it, perhaps you shouldn't be doing this kind of interview.

Getting the style right

"The hardest part for beginners is getting the style right," a commissioning editor at *Bella* told me. At the time of writing, the same publication has no fewer than four full-time commissioning editors. Their job is not only to buy human interest features but to rewrite them in the style of the magazine.

One of the biggest challenges for beginners is how to open the story. Study the style of your chosen market carefully. You'll see that in many publications you should pick a focal point and progress the story from there. Let's look at the story I wrote about the woman with the sandwich board. I felt the most moving part of this story was this poor woman out on the street, so that's where I began:

> Aileen Cohen glanced at her watch before taking up her position outside Bond Street underground station in London's West End. It was 8.15 a.m., about the time when thousands of office workers would spill out of the Tube making their way to work.

Your focal point could be the middle of the story, or a dramatic point which brings the story to life. Now go to the beginning of the story – the time when she is made redundant. Tell the story chronologically and in a logical progression. Details add the human touch and help the reader empathise with the character. Here are the details I included about the sandwich lady.

> Aileen stapled clear film over her board to protect it from the rain, and for safety, she carried a money belt. In it were cards showing her name and address, her keys, travelcard, some small change and a hanky.

But how did your character *feel* when the events of the story were happening? Your writing should be full of quotations and not only from the heroine of the story. Study the style of the magazine carefully and if a quotation from a third party is always included, that's what you should do, too. In some cases, you may need to hear from Mum, Dad, Auntie, Granny and whoever else is involved. Let's say a young schoolgirl has rescued a neighbour's baby from a fire. You need to hear from the grateful mother, the fire officer, perhaps even from the girl's headteacher. Get their reactions.

In writing up your story, you should also inject a feeling of atmosphere and setting. A man hanging off a cliff face in biting cold is more dramatic than the same fellow suffering in warm sunshine. As the story of Aileen took place outside, I asked her what it was like standing there when the weather turned nasty:

> "On cold wet days, office workers would send me cups of coffee. They said they'd help if they could but they had no vacancies."

From the editor's point of view, it's most important that you get all the facts and tie up the loose ends. Accuracy is everything. Get ages, names, the names of hospitals, the names of the local magistrates' court. Be sure to get your timings right: this happened in February, then that happened in June.

Good human interest writers inject exactly the right element of warmth, pathos and drama into their work. They also remember to tell a story. Your best training ground is cup of coffee in hand, feet up, reading other people's published stories.

Where beginners go wrong – editors speak out

If human interest features are so demanding to write, what should novices watch out for? I asked two editors experienced in commissioning such stories what are the commonest mistakes made by beginners. They listed:

● lack of impact with the opening
● getting the time-scale muddled
● writing personal reminiscence
● leaving out key facts and information

"A common mistake is a slow and rambling beginning," says Dee Remmington, former assistant editor of *Woman* and also ex-features editor of *Woman's Own*. "Don't tell the story in the first paragraph but start off in a way that makes people want to read on. At some point you must state your case."

She continues, "Muddling up times is another fault. A flash-back within a flashback, so you get completely muddled up – are we talking about today, 20 years ago or five years before then? Instead, pose the question right at the beginning: 'What does a mother do when she finds out her son is gay?' Then take the story through logically and chronologically from beginning to end."

"And if you're going to tell a story, tell a story – not a catalogue of woes, disasters and medical operations," points out Lesley Dobson, former assistant editor (features) of *Bella*. "Not 'and then his leg fell off and then his arm fell off and then his brother died . . .' Make the story flow."

According to Lesley Dobson, there's another common reason for rejection. "The worst thing – and this will get your story sent straight back to you – is to write in a personal style, telling your own story. Beginners sit down and think 'I could write about my time in the War' and they write about it. Very few magazines want the writer to be in the feature. You have to write from outside and to style."

Does all this sound very daunting? Take heart. If you have included enough vital facts and details, the magazine's own staff writers will be able to complete the finishing touches and you'll

33

earn your full fee. The important factor is to leave no vital gaps in your information. The reader should never be left wondering "whatever happened to her Uncle John in the end?" Don't leave key questions unanswered.

Dee Remmington tells the story of a beginner writer who interviewed her next-door neighbour. It was the story of a 30-year-old woman whose hair turned white and fell out within about a week. One of the obvious questions the beginner forgot to ask at the interview was "Have you had any terrible shocks lately?" Never be afraid to ask the obvious.

Make sure you're got everything you need, make sure it's accurate, get spellings of names, ages, find out what they do and find out times between events. If you've got all the information, then the magazine can do something with it. It may feel difficult at the time but it's even more difficult going back again and again to the interviewee. Don't be surprised if magazine editors phone you months after you've submitted the piece for small details you've left out.

In summary, if you are a good writer, have a feel for words and are not afraid to go back and try again, you can write and sell your human interest features. The important part is to read enough copies of the target magazine. Magazines have an insatiable need for good human interest features so they need your work. I sold the first human interest feature I ever wrote.

4

CELEBRITY INTERVIEWS

There is one type of interview easier to sell than any other. It pays more and can be sold all over the world. Specialise in celebrity interviews and you can virtually name your price. It's not easy to break into this market but if other people can, why not you?

What is a celebrity?

A celebrity is a "famous person" and when we use this term we normally mean a person in showbusiness. In this book, I'll talk about interviews with stage, screen or radio personalities because that's where my experience lies. But for the purposes of selling your profiles, the celebrity could also be: a well-known author, artist, film director, sportsman, church leader or politician. You could talk to an ordinary person who temporarily becomes famous or even notorious, for example, an actress who has an affair with a famous politician, which causes him to resign. All would produce a celebrity interview which you could sell.

The market for celebrity interviews is staggering. If I told you I'm addicted to Bounty bars and consequently need to lose ten pounds, it would be boring. If I were a celebrity, on the other hand, somebody somewhere would pay for and publish that information. The most saleable story of all is the celebrity human interest feature (example: a star tells of her fight to adopt a child). But there are numerous markets – from teen magazines to quality Sunday papers – hanging out for the merest tidbits of information.

The more people find your chosen celebrity famous, the more markets you have for a potential sale. This is why top-earning journalists who specialise in this field define a celebrity as *someone whose interview you can sell in more than one country*. This is where you'll reap the largest rewards by selling separate rights to the interview in several different countries. (More about this in Chapter 10.)

Does this mean if you want to enter this field you have to get hold of international tennis stars or hot Hollywood heart-throbs? No. Fortunately for the beginner, the term celebrity has become open to wide interpretation. Let me give you an example. The other night I was watching a so-called celebrity quiz on TV. I found that out of the panel I recognised only one or two faces. It is in this grey area of who is and isn't a celebrity that your opportunities lie. What matters is that the person you choose is *famous to the readers of your chosen market*.

Realistic goals

In celebrity interviewing – sorry to admit this in a writer's guide – your ability to secure the interview is more important than your ability to write. When preparing this book, I spoke to a director of one of Britain's leading celebrity features agencies. He put it as bluntly as this: "If you can get yourself on to the set of (insert name of hot Hollywood star)'s latest movie, with (insert name of hottest director in town) directing, and get an exclusive interview – even if you were illiterate, you'd be able to sell it."

The traditional path into celebrity interviewing is via a staff job in the features department of a magazine or on the showbiz pages of a national newspaper. But if you're not a trained journalist and don't have the weight of a paper behind you, your procedure as a freelance will be:

- land those interviews by hook or by crook – see below
- prove to editors that you've got what it takes by sending in a number of interviews, to length, on time

36

- having proved yourself, get a commission from the publication to talk to bigger names

As a beginner, you must be realistic. If Jane Fonda waltzes into town, it won't be a matter of which magazine wants to talk to her, but to whom she decides to talk. Go for celebrities with whom you're more likely to get an interview. If you're not sure what I mean, let's for a moment divide famous people into categories.

- Megastars – the likes of Michael Jackson, Diana Ross, Elizabeth Taylor as well as those in current Hollywood movies. The easiest to sell but you're unlikely to get the interview
- TV Soap Stars – remembered by the public while the soap is on
- Middlestars – temporarily famous because on TV at the moment
- Former Film Stars – not doing much at the moment but resting on past glories
- Sundries (sorry, chaps!) – TV cooks, weatherpersons, presenters
- Oldtimer Showbiz Greats – they've been in the business for ever, are secure in their fame but not particularly hot from the editor's point of view
- Rising Stars – likely to give you the interview but hard to sell to editors

I've placed the top category apart for a reason. You have two problems with your interview: getting the person to talk to you and getting the editor interested. It's a Catch 22. A Megastar is easy to sell but hard to secure for the interview. A Rising Star is easier to get, but hard to sell to editors. In the middle ground, as you can see from the list above, there are people who are quite easy to get, in whom editors are also interested.

So if you dream of selling your profile with a major star to *GQ*, *Elle* or the *Sunday Times*, be patient a while. To break in as a unknown freelance, you'll need first to get into print and then to build up your contacts and reputation.

The publicity machine

The world of showbiz relies on publicity. Why? Because it has a cycle. Films, TV and radio programmes, plays and operas come up on a regular basis and need exposure. One option for the film and TV companies would be to spend thousands of pounds on advertising. But why bother when they can get free advertising by getting their stars into the papers? And that means an interview with you.

Celebrities will talk to you when they have something *to plug*. The plug or publicity angle is the part which appears beneath the interview saying:

> Mervin Megastar's latest movie, the thriller *Golden Vest*, opens in London on 4th June.

The plug will not necessarily be anything to do with the subject of the feature. For example, a star might show you around his holiday hideaway for an article in a women's magazine and, at the end, you'll mention his new film.

The plug gives your article the topical hook editors will be looking for. It makes even less famous people more interesting. Not many magazines would be interested in a Rising Star actress, say, but she'll be a saleable celebrity for as long as she's in a current television programme.

In the example above, where the new movie opens in early June, your profile would fit best in a May or June issue. Remember the advice about timing in Chapter 1? This means submitting to a monthly magazine four to six months in advance of the date to be published. This leads us to your next problem. How will you get the advance information you need that Mervin Megastar is making a film at all?

The answer is to approach the press officers of film, opera and theatre production companies, TV channels and radio stations. (If you have decided to profile famous authors, you'd write to publishers.)

When approaching press departments, be bold. Appear to be a specialist – even if you aren't yet. So if you are approaching a TV channel, say, identify your area of expertise as *light entertainment*, and ask for the person dealing with that area. Request "advance programme information" for the next few "seasons". You could say that you've been "asked by a couple of magazines to put up ideas for profiles".

Don't be humble. The publicity machine needs you. Press officers are paid to make celebrities accessible to journalists, in return you're giving their programmes free exposure. For the celebrity too, the deal cuts two ways. To secure the plug, they must be prepared to give you an interesting interview.

Good beginners' markets

Having identified that some celebrities will be more approachable than others, let's look at good opportunities for the novice. The overwhelming majority of celebrity interviews appear in what I've called *regular slots*. A slot is a feature which has the same number of words, formula and theme every week. It could be a short paragraph in a TV magazine on the subject of *My TV Dinner* or 1000 words on a theme such as *The Way I Was*.

In regular slots, the theme is always the same but the celebrity changes, so it's vital to do your homework. Let's say the theme is *Me and My Health*. If Mike Middlestar plans to talk to you about giving up smoking, check whether the magazine has already tackled this particular health problem. You may need a different crisis (appendicitis, say) or a different market. (This may be easier than it sounds. On the subject of *Me and My Health* alone, I have seen celebrity slots in the *Evening Standard*, *Here's Health* and *TV Quick* to name but three. I've even seen a slot entitled *Me and My Operation*!)

Don't go for the obvious markets, but think laterally and do your research. Perhaps you read by chance that Mike Middlestar doesn't eat meat. Could you interview him for *Vegetarian Living*? Find out that a star owns an unusual breed of dog and you may have the basis of a piece for *Dogs Today*.

Local magazines – *Southern Life*, *Cheshire Life*, etc. – are another good market for the beginner. Your celebrity lives in the area covered by the magazine *and* has a new book coming out? Opportunity knocks.

Round-ups

A good interview option for the beginner is the celebrity round-up. A round-up is a selection of opinions rounded up for your feature. For example, in the *News of the World Sunday* magazine, a journalist asked seven celebrities to describe their recurrent dreams. A psychologist then commented on what each person's dream might signify.

Let's look what you would have to do to write this round-up. First you'd suggest the idea to the editor indicating the personalities you intend to quiz. The celebrities must be faces the readers recognise. Next you'll approach the celebrities and question them either face to face, in writing or on the phone. You will speak to many more people than appear in your article. Why? Some will not be able to remember their dreams; some will choose not to be involved; still others will be helpful but have a dull dream to relate.

A round-up article can take months to prepare and the seven comments that appear on the page may seem little compared to the effort you put in. You may not consider such interviews real writing. Nevertheless, it's an excellent training ground. While getting your final seven comments, you'll make many contacts for future use. In one such project I tackled, the showbiz editor of the publication supplied most of the telephone numbers. Editors know how much patient telephoning is involved and that's why you're more likely, as a freelance, to get the commission. Last, but certainly not least, such interviews pay well. For the first celebrity round-up I sold, I earned several hundreds of pounds plus telephone expenses.

In the *News of the World Sunday* magazine example I chose, a balance of three men and four women relate their dreams. They are not big names: four TV presenters, two minor actors and one DJ. The feature doesn't even have a topical hook. Despite what

I've said about being topical, celebrity pieces are so saleable this may be one rule you can break.

How to track down famous people

The right way to approach a celebrity is the way that works for you. Much depends on your personal ethics and style. I wouldn't dream of looking an actor up in the phone book and calling him at home. But I might hand in a friendly letter at the stage door of the theatre where he was appearing.

One of the easiest ways to land your first celebrity interview is through a contact. Consider your job. Are you an actress, sound engineer, studio secretary, stage manager, musician, showbiz solicitor or in any way connected with showbiz? My background is in advertising copywriting and during my career I made frequent radio commericials. In this way, I came to meet many actors and actresses who performed the voice-overs.

What about your friends, colleagues and family? Did your boss go to school with Mike Middlestar? It might be the magic connection that lands you the appointment.

If you've no contacts whatever, approach celebrities via their agent. To find out who represents whom, phone Spotlight on 0171 437 7631 or look through the Spotlight directory (7 Leicester Place, London WC2H 7BP) which you'll find at good reference libraries. There are separate directories for actors and actresses and underneath the black-and-white photo, you'll find the person's agent with address and phone number.

When ringing agents, it's vital to sound confident and professional. Using the right jargon will ensure you're not given the brush-off in the first five minutes. Don't say: "Are you the agent for Matt Fame?" but "Can I speak to the person who looks after Matt Fame?" Many agents represent numerous stars so you need to speak directly to the person handling that person. To boost your confidence, do as much research as possible before making your call. You should know that actor X is rehearsing Y at the National Theatre or what part actress B plays in *EastEnders*.

Many agents will ask you to put the details of your request in writing – over the fax, if possible. Although this may sound ponderous, it's worthwhile. If you're more confident on paper, than over the phone (I know I am), you'll have time to present your case in the best light possible. Some agents may ask you to put the questions in writing. While this may seem like a good idea, it gives the celebrity plenty of time to sort out a laundered and artificial-sounding reply. Far better if you can phone them or they you at a convenient moment. A good tip is to ask agents for a full list of the other celebrities they represent. That way if you strike a good relationship with a particular agent, you may be able to interview some other names on their books.

Much more helpful than agents are publicists and press officers who have a job to do promoting either the celebrity or, more commonly, a specific programme or production. If you're on the mailing lists, sooner or later, you'll be invited to the launch of a new book or programme. Phone up and find out who's coming. Some of the key personalities may be available for photographers and journalists on the day. This is known as a photocall.

Once a magazine is confident in your ability to write the piece (you've written two or three for them) they may ask you to *chase* celebrities for them. In Fig. 4 on p 114, there is a letter I wrote to an agent when I knew the magazine was prepared to commission the feature. Note how I reassure the agent that there's a plug, and tell her exactly what is involved.

How to sell celebrity interviews

One of the commonest questions asked by beginners is "Whom should I approach first – the celebrity or the magazine?" Unless you are selling a *big star* – in my experience, it's wise to check first that the celebrity is suitable for the intended market – nothing is more embarrassing than persuading a personality to talk to you for Magazine X then finding that the magazine isn't interested.

Never tell a lie but you don't have to tell the whole truth. "I'll be seeing Frances Middlestar next week and wondered if you'd be interested in an interview for the My Favourite Outfit section?" If you do this by phone, you haven't committed yourself in writing and the angle is obvious. As the interview is being offered on spec only, the editor is not making any kind of commitment.

Editors have specific ideas as to which celebrities interest their readers. The showbiz editor of a TV weekly made it clear that he wanted faces the reader might have seen on a Wednesday evening on ITV between 8 and 10 p.m. If your market is a glossy women's monthly magazine, you might check whether the male celebrities featured tend to be good-looking and fanciable. If when you mention the name, the editor says "Who?" you need to elaborate. Some people have very well known faces but their names are not so easily remembered. David Suchet would be much more quickly identified if you said Poirot. The next question the editor will ask is, "What's so-and-so doing at the moment?" – the topical hook. Answer: "She has a new series starting in March on BBC 2."

After that, if the editor says yes, approach your second potential market. If you like, this time you can insert the name of the other magazine. "I'll be interviewing Frances Middlestar for *Woman's Realm* next week and wonder if you'd be interested in her for XYZ slot." But never tell lies either to celebrity or to magazine. Don't say it's a commission if it isn't. They may check with the magazine. Use phrases like "I propose to offer this to *Best*" or "*Best* has expressed firm interest in an interview".

Make sure the magazine hasn't run the celebrity before. A friend of mine did several interviews for a local magazine and was confident he knew what was needed. Once, when the editor was away, he interviewed a local celebrity without getting the go-ahead first. But the person had already been in the magazine! "Why didn't the celebrity speak up?" you may ask. Well, some people do hundreds of interviews and rely on their agent to sort it all out. It's up to you to do your homework.

You'll note with everything I've said here that the risk is all on your side. If you line up two or three interviews with the famous person, and write them all, you will be very unlucky not to make a sale.

Developing a speciality

One way to break in is to develop a speciality. William Cook is a freelance writer who discovered in the early 80s that while many journalists were writing about theatre, few knew much about comedy. So he became an expert, establishing a reputation not only for good writing but also for sound judgment. Soon the *Scotsman* sent him to interview Barry Humphries, Gary Glitter and Shirley MacLaine; today William is comedy critic for the *Guardian*. He landed his first interview like this:

"Before the Edinburgh Festival, the different venues launch their programmes in London. I went along to the Pleasance which is one of the best places for young comedians to get started and I arranged to interview a novelty act called Earl Okin. It wasn't commissioned. I sold this and another interview to the *Scotsman*, then went up to Edinburgh and did reviews for them."

It was selling to the *Scotsman*, he reckons, which was his big break. "Although they had both a London theatre and an art critic, they had nobody picking up the odd stories. It was quite easy to get interviews – Scottish artists showing in London, Scottish actors in West End plays." Note that one of William's tips is to spot a gap in the market and he suggests "If you don't (like me) live in the capital, why not get material about the regions and get it into London papers?"

Develop an expertise and trust your judgment. "If you think someone's good and they are unknown, it's never a waste of time going to see them," says William who followed comedian Jack Dee from when he was a complete unknown. The first sale was a review for *City Limits* (London listings magazine). After an interview and feature on Jack Dee in Edinburgh for the same magazine, pieces for the *Scotsman* and the *Guardian* followed. "The last thing I did with him was a 3000 word cover story in *For Him*, the men's monthly, half-a-dozen pages between photos. It was a much better interview because I know his background."

William's experiences contain several valuable tips on how to break in. One way to make a name for yourself when talking to the much-interviewed is to uncover something no-one else knows. You'll do this in two ways: by scrupulous research (see the next chapter) and by your ability to gain trust and establish a rapport.

In recent years, the celebrity's trust in journalists has been stretched to the limit. One actress who has been interviewed hundreds of times told me. "The mark of a good interviewer is someone who gets people sufficiently relaxed to say more than they were going to and to believe it's not going to be used against them." I think that sums it up neatly.

5

PREPARING FOR THE INTERVIEW

In Chapter 1, we discussed the types of people you could interview. Two such categories are experts and the person-in-the street.
To talk to them, you'll first have to find them. The professional
writer not only knows where to find information but, if necessary,
can act like a detective.

How to find experts

Let's return to the article I wrote on non-smoking restaurants and
pubs in London (described in Chapter 1). To research this feature,
I needed to speak to a representative of an official body, such as
Action on Smoking and Health (ASH). Where to find him or her?

Since ASH is quite a well-known organisation, I looked up the
number in the phone book. But had I not known the appropriate
organisation, one book I would have found helpful is the *Directory of British Associations (DBA)* to be found in good libraries.
Under the subject index, I would have looked up the word *smoking*. A number of organisations is listed – from the Freedom
Organisation for the Right to Enjoy Smoking Tobacco (FOREST)
to the Association for Non-smokers' Rights. What is particularly
useful here is that there are bodies representing both points of
view. My next step would be to phone and ask to speak to the
press officer.

For the same article on smoke-free restaurants, I needed to speak
to the press officer for McDonald's. Find press contacts in *Hollis*

Press & Public Relations Annual published annually by Hollis Directories, Sunbury on Thames, Middlesex.

Official organisations, support groups and charities will be a source not only of experts but of suitable interviewees for triumph over tragedy features. *Take A Break* published the sad story of a man who contracted Alzheimer's Disease in his early forties. It is very likely the journalist found the family to interview by contacting the Alzheimer's Disease Society.

For the more ambitious human interest story, you will need to do quite a bit of research. Let's imagine a block of flats collapsed in Manchester six months ago and you'd like to interview a family who'd survived the disaster. Your first step would be to refer to the newspaper coverage of the time. You could contact the *Manchester Evening News* and find out if they have a cuttings service i.e. will look out back issues for you for a small fee. Find the address in *The Writer's Handbook* (Macmillan/PEN).

Next check the *Social Services Year Book* (Longman) which is available in larger libraries. Look up the addresses of two other bodies who may be able to help. These are: the local police constabulary (ask for the press officer) and the Department of Social Services (contact Director of Social Services). Police and social services are often involved in setting up post-disaster helplines and counselling and may be able to put you in touch with families involved.

Researching celebrities

The more you know about a celebrity, the more likely you are to find a new and unique angle for the interview. Where do you go for that information?

Start with the person's agent or publicist. Most will send you a biography and some will provide cuttings. Be warned, they may assume you have a fax machine. Don't expect miracles. While some agents will send off an entertaining two pages or so, detailing the person's hobbies and best moments, others reduce the c.v. to a list of dates: 1988 *Bladerunner*, 1991 *Bladerunner 2*. You should also remember that other writers wanting to interview Mervin Megastar will get the same list. So angles suggested by the c.v. are not likely to be the most original – and c.v.s can be out of date.

Other sources of information are your friends, your clippings files (see Chapter 2) and the agent. A helpful publicist can also tip you off as to which subjects the celebrity prefers not to talk about. Occasionally, they will provide up to the minute gossip such as "she's about to get engaged".

A surprising amount of information is available free in a good reference library. Let's try looking up the film star Susannah York for example. By referring to *Who's Who* (A & C Black), I discovered that she has a son and a daughter and her hobbies include languages. In *Quinlan's Illustrated Directory of Film Stars* (Batsford), I learnt that she is a writer of children's books. *Screen International Film & Television Yearbook* told me she has appeared on *The Two Ronnies*. If you live in or near London you might consider the British Film Institute Library and Information Services (21 Stephen Street, London W1P 2LN, 0171 255 1444) or the Independent Television Commission library (33 Foley Street, London W1P 7LB, 0171 255 3000).

If, through a lucky break, you land an interview with a big star, you might be prepared to pay a professional information bureau to do a *search* for you. It costs money but could be a worthwhile investment. At the beginning of your career, the clipping of the interview you sold is important because it gives you something to show editors.

Taking notes

There are three methods you could use to take notes: you can trust to memory; take written notes; or use a tape recorder. I've met journalists who rely entirely on memory. While this might be good enough for a quick survey of, say, Mums in a toy shop, it really isn't a practical option for an hour-long interview. My memory can be notoriously unreliable and what I've committed to paper can be the very opposite of what the person actually said.

There are many instances, too, where you want to quote EXACTLY what was said. Interviewing an intelligent, highly outspoken actress, I found that every remark she came out with was a "quotable quote". In cases where you are interviewing experts, also, and particularly when you haven't the foggiest what they are talking about, you must get it down correctly. This brings us to shorthand. If you're lucky enough to have mastered this skill, you'll certainly find it useful. I wish I had learnt. If not, you might try a simplified version such as leaving out vowels to give *thk* instead of *think*, *u* instead of *you*. Shorthand will save you the bother of typing up your tapes later but has several disadvantages. It can hold up the flow as the person pauses politely to let you finish scribbling. You will also be a less active listener if you're constantly buried in your note pad. Finally, it can offend if you appear to find some remarks worth noting, others not.

A tape recorder, on the other hand, lets you edit at your leisure. My vote is for the tape recorder plus notes and my Sony has never let me down. Put it within easy reach of the person's voice, test after a few minutes, then try to forget about it if you can. While listening attentively, take a few notes of key points and mark with an asterisk. This will save you valuable time later when typing up your tape. It is only good manners to ask if you may use a recorder. I phrase this positively. "I'd hate to misquote you on anything so I trust you don't mind me using a tape recorder." Most people forget about the recorder after a while and talk quite naturally. It helps if you relax rather than glance nervously at your recorder every second or so to check it's still turning.

If you want to record a telephone conversation, you will need a telephone listening device. I bought mine from Berry's of Holborn, 37 High Holborn, London WC1. Good electrical shops which sell small tape recorders should be able to help you. It is illegal to tape telephone conversations unless you tell the interviewee what you are doing. Explain that it's because your note-taking simply isn't fast enough or that you'd hate to misquote the person. Typing up your notes from your tape afterwards is time-consuming. If you have a tight deadline, you may have to take notes instead of a recorder. In important interviews, notes *and* a recorder is the only safe option.

49

Interviewing by telephone

Earlier in this book, I said that an interview is "a conversation between two people for the purposes of gaining information". So why couldn't you do that over the phone? In practice, Alexander Graham Bell's invention has several disadvantages: we are used to employing it for short periods to exchange facts so, in a phone interview, you and the other person will tire much more quickly. On the telephone, you cannot smooth things over with body language. Nor can you use your sense of smell, touch, sight or taste to gain an impression of the other person and his surroundings. Worst of all, the telephone interrupts routine so people have no time to gather their thoughts. But here's where you'll use it to best advantage:

● for preliminary interviewing, to check that there really is enough here to make a story. Particularly useful when you are researching human interest interviews.

● for getting facts and opinions from experts, doctors, scientists, press officers. You don't need more than quarter of an hour.

● for canvassing opinions as in the round-up type of interview (discussed in Chapter 2). But read my note about this below.

● when that's the only way you'll get to talk to the person at all.

You can't see interviewees and they can't see you on the telephone. Sometimes this can be an advantage – where the interview becomes like a confessional. A colleague of mine who specialises in human interest features was researching a subject of a very delicate nature. The only way she could persuade a certain couple to talk to her was on the telephone, names changed to ensure total privacy. She didn't know where they lived or where they were phoning from. "I like working on the phone," she told me. "Everything is concentrated in your voice and theirs."

You can't see them and they can't see you. This is why the celebrity interview by phone is a waste of time. Readers are less interested in Meryl Megastar's political views than in whether her eyes really are green – the personal, gossipy side. Is she as gorgeous as you expected or fatter, older, more wrinkled?

There is a natural length to a telephone conversation and there are certain things people don't tell you. "Nobody's ever told me a funny story on the phone," revealed comedy critic, William Cook. "They're not sufficiently relaxed." This is why the face-to-face will always beat the chin-to-receiver. Even when doing a round-up interview, I recommend you meet at least two of the subjects in person. Your finished feature will be richer for it.

Ten tips on telephone technique

Your first contact with most interviewees will be by telephone. Your manner and voice can make or break the relationship. If you're nervous, rude, overbearing or abrasive, you may never get the interview. Here are ten tried and tested tips for getting better mileage out of the "dog and bone".

1. Be courteous and ring people at reasonable hours. You know how irritating it is to be called by that double-glazing sales-person when you're in the middle of eating dinner. The only person you can phone very late is the rock star you *know* stays up all night.
2. Develop an instinct for when your call is interrupting some-thing. Offer to ring back when it is more convenient. But don't leave this open – make a telephone appointment. "May I ring you back at 7, then?" Stick to the time agreed and phone on the dot. This shows not only that you're consider-ate but that you mean business. The only time I break this rule is when I've been chasing someone for weeks. In that case, if I'm lucky enough to get her on the end of a phone, I strike while the iron is hot.
3. Where time allows, give experts and scientists advance warn-ing of your call. This way, they'll have a couple of days to

research the subject and have far more information to give you.

4. Where a third party has put you in touch, mention the name of the contact person as soon as possible in the conversation. "Mary Smith of ABC suggested I contact you about XYZ." This allays the fear that you're a salesperson.

5. Take a tip from actors. Make your voice warmer and more friendly by using "smile" – literally smiling as you speak. Even if you've had a lousy morning, force yourself to crack your face. It works.

6. If intimidated about the person you're approaching, or you want to sound more confident, try making the phone call standing up. If very nervous, write down a script which you've rehearsed with a good friend. If you want to sound more relaxed, perhaps you could try phoning while you're lying on the couch. This is a friend's tip, by the way, not tested by me. I prefer the smile technique.

7. I like to call other people, rather than have them call me back. For a tricky scientific subject, it can take all your mental powers to get to grips with the material. I once made a telephone appointment with a hospital consultant who forgot the appointment, then phoned me back out of the blue some hours later. I was not prepared, floundered around and was not able to absorb the complex scientific facts. Moral: if expecting a very busy person to call you back, keep a pad and a note of *exactly* what you want to ask by the phone.

8. Don't go silent at your end of the receiver. This sounds cold and as if you're not listening. Keep contact with an occasional "Yes, is that so? Mmm," to remind them you're still there and eager for more.

9. If a person can't help you with a piece of information, ask for the name and, if possible, the number of someone else who can. This way your call won't be wasted and you'll expand the network of interviewees for your article.

10. When the call is over, emphasise that everything the person has told you has been helpful and interesting. If you think it will reassure the person, leave your name and telephone number.

Fixing the time/place/day

Which are you, a lark or an owl? I can't imagine anything worse than trying to chat up a night owl at nine in the morning. So, when fixing an interview appointment, I always ask the person which time of day *he* would prefer. The interviewee's preferences come before your own: if a factory manager wants to see you at 8 a.m. or a rock star at 11 p.m, you'll simply have to be there. In the case of elderly people, be considerate; if quizzing a busy parent, try to choose a time when the children aren't around.

When it comes to the place, it depends on what you're writing. For a celebrity piece, the ideal location is the star's own home if you're lucky enough to be invited. A personal environment reveals much more than a sterile hotel room. What kind of soap does Meryl Megastar have in the loo? Is her sitting-room really all in white? You would never have believed she made her own chutney but the evidence is all there on the kitchen counter. The next best thing is a personalised environment such as a theatre dressing-room or a person's office.

It's up to you to suggest the venue? Choose somewhere congenial, where you're unlikely to be distracted and you can use your tape recorder with minimum background noise. That pub, wine bar or café may seem perfect until you hear the whooshing espresso machine, loud muzak or echoing floor. If possible, do a recce first and check that Juan the guitarist isn't due to start his act ten minutes into your conversation.

Should you interview over a meal or a couple of pints out with the lads? It depends on you and the other person. Unless you're very self-possessed, have sophisticated recording equipment and a good head for liquor, I'd say leave that for later when you've a little more experience. For all these reasons I prefer the comfortable, well-carpeted foyers of upmarket hotels.

That's the interview time and place. The right day to make the interview is as soon as possible after getting the commission. If someone's good enough to grant you an interview, don't give him a chance to change his mind. So if he offers you Tuesday, Wednesday or Thursday, take Tuesday.

Your interview survival kit

Outward bound fiends will know an expedition works better if you remember all the equipment. That means not just tent, comfortable shoes and a rucksack but also tent pegs, torch, sun tan oil and mosquito repellent. Forget any item on the list and you're going to suffer. The same applies to the interview survival kit.

The first essential you'll need is something to carry it all in. I use a cross between a briefcase and handbag, a kind of large leather bag with zip compartments and a shoulder strap. Any kind of large shoulder bag will do. It helps if your bag is large enough to keep A4 documents without creasing, because one thing I'm going to take is a copy of the publication for whom I'm doing the interview. Reading this *en route* to the interview reminds me of the kind of article I'm about to write and what the reader wants to know. Take also a copy of any other item you want to discuss such as the author's new book or a controversial press cutting plus, of course, your list of questions (see Chapter 6).

Next into my bag goes my bright red hard-backed A5 work book. In a longer feature involving many interviews and much research, it is dangerous and impractical to write notes down on scraps of paper. My workbook is solid and red and I know if I'm missing a scrap of information, it'll be in there somewhere. Some writers recommend a separate exercise book for each feature.

You're going to be taking notes so you'll need a sharp pencil or two, pencil sharpener or if you prefer, a biro. The important thing is that your writing instrument will fly across the page.

Next into my bag goes my battery-operated Sony tape recorder with C90 tape in situ and marked with the date and name of the interviewee. This prevents you taping over this by accident at a later date. Always check that tape recorder is turning and batteries are live. (A good precaution is to chuck all batteries immediately once dead.) After that, you're on to back-up equipment: spare batteries, spare tape, spare battery or mains-operated tape recorder.

Why so cautious? One reason is that there are those celebrities so nervous of the press they like to make their own tape of the proceedings. A spare tape recorder allows you to offer them this facility. The other reason is fear of mechanical failure – your tape recorder jamming.

Will you be taking pictures? Don't forget your camera equipment, plenty of film and spare camera battery.

A business card helps to reassure interviewees that you're professional. If you don't feel you're at that stage yet, keep a few sticky-backed name and address labels in your wallet. Order them from Able-Label, Steepleprint Ltd., Earls Barton, Northampton NN6 0LS.

A successful friend of mine asks himself "Where? How? What?" before leaving for interviews. "Where am I going? How am I getting there? What are we discussing?" Please don't laugh but I have in the past been so preoccupied with thinking about the interview that I left home without the person's address. Take address, map, telephone number, and enough funds for a taxi if you're delayed. I wish you a successful expedition.

6

QUESTION TIME

If ten different people were sent to talk to a famous star, they would all come back with different interviews. Success as an interviewer depends, more than anything else, on the ability to establish rapport and ask the right questions. The more thoughtful your questions, the better your interview.

How to prepare your questions

Why prepare questions at all? If being a good interviewer is all about establishing rapport, why not simply get together with your interviewee for an enjoyable chat? There's a great deal to be said for a relaxed approach but consider the disadvantages. You come back with masses of information about the person's new hobby of bee-keeping but nothing on his new book. Or in the case of the celebrity seeking publicity, that's the only thing he talks about. (When you try to see the interviewee again to get more information, he's not available.) Or what happens if you both get an attack of nerves and dry up?

Seasoned interviewers may advocate the bareback approach but don't believe for a minute they go into the ring without careful preparation. When you're new to interviewing, a list of questions is essential – if only to boost your confidence.

Having a set of questions ensures you cover everything you need to know. When you're on a brief, fact-finding mission, (see telephone interviews, Chapter 5), it's particularly important to get the crucial questions over. Think of your feature as a complex recipe and the list of questions as your shopping list. Taking a list means you won't forget any of the vital ingredients.

Of course, a great cook doesn't stick to the recipe. As you talk, you'll go off at a tangent and discover new ingredients you hadn't expected. But your list will ensure you get enough to make a cake.

The finished article should tell a story with a beginning, middle and end. So your questions, too, should have a logical sequence: you could start with the background, proceed to what the person is currently doing (the new or topical part), and then end with asking about future plans.

Your market and angle determine the questions. I can't over-emphasise the importance of market study. Know what kind of readers you're writing for and ask yourself what they'd want to know. This will vary widely. For example, readers of *Mizz* might want to know if an actress was ever fat or suffered from "zits" as a teenager; *Woman's Journal* readers what she thinks about HRT, face-lifts and second marriages. You're interviewing a managing director about a new grant for businesses? The readers – other business people – want to know where to apply, how much you get, how the company intends to use the money.

Whenever I'm preparing questions, I get hold of as many similar pieces from the publication as possible. When preparing a *Me and My Health* celebrity piece for a TV magazine, I noticed that in every example, a celebrity told of some health crisis that affected his career or childhood. So I ensured that most of my questions related to health, starting with the simple "What was your health like as a child?" moving on to more creative questions "Have you ever had to lose weight for a role?"

What you're trying to achieve is a good piece of writing. So use your imagination and explore every area till you strike lucky. One actor I interviewed is short-sighted but rarely wears his glasses on camera. So I asked "Is it a problem if you ever have to do a stunt without your glasses?" This question prompted some fascinating stories. A thoughtful approach can work for you, too.

Essential questions

There is no standard type of interview. But there are some questions which always apply. Check with the interviewee how she spells her name. Get it wrong and you'll not only irritate the person, you'll instantly stamp yourself as unprofessional. "But won't the magazine do that for me?" you ask. Don't count on it. Although the quality magazines and press have whole armies of sub-editors (people whose job it is to check for spelling and factual accuracy), smaller publications do not. I have lost count of the number of times my own by-line, Jayne with a y, has been spelt incorrectly, without the y. Take particular care with names that seem obvious: Anne (with or without an e?), Sarah (with an h?), Graham (or Graeme?).

Next step is to include some questions which relate to background. You may know the expression "It's not the getting there, it's the journey". *How* a person came to be doing what they are doing is the most interesting part of the story. Examples: the Prime Minister who left school at 16 and comes from a circus family; the loony comedian who trained to be a barrister; the rags-to-riches story. In human interest interviews (see Chapter 3), the background adds to the build-up of emotion. You're writing about a couple whose only child died of a rare disease? Ask them how they met and fell in love. Did they always long for children?

Parents and siblings have enormous influence on what we grow up to be. So find out about the interviewee's mother and father, brothers and sisters. Warren Beatty's half-sister is Shirley MacLaine. Does your subject have any interesting relatives? So intriguing can the relationship be that the *Sunday Times* magazine has a regular slot devoted to it, entitled "Relative Values".

Readers are also fascinated by family background so get as many details as you can. This is particularly important for the women's market. Ms X may be brilliantly successful in her career, but is she so successful with men? asks the reader. How does handsome actor Y keep his marriage strong when he's constantly shooting scenes with beautiful women? Are there any children and, if so, give names and ages. In some cases, the person's partner is all-important to her story – where would Anita Roddick be without

Gordon? Does a person have a mentor?

Next on your list are questions covering the so-called topical hook. (We discussed this in Chapter 2. Editors need a reason for taking your material *now*.) In TV interviews this is the rather embarrassing bit where the interviewer says "Tell me about your new show/book/film." In an interview with a successful entrepreneur you might ask "What makes setting up a new business in the middle of a recession particularly tough?" Let's say a new law has been set up banning smoking in public places. Ask smokers/non-smokers "How will the new law affect you?".

All the time you should be phrasing your questions in a way likely to bring on a fuller story or anecdote. Don't just ask "Do funny things ever happen on the show?", ask for examples.

References to the future give your profile an upbeat note and take the material onwards, so ask where the interviewee is going next. A 35-year-old woman adopted at birth meets her other sisters and brothers for the first time. Ask her what the coming Christmas will be like with the new family. Are there any plans to meet other relatives?

How to write open-ended questions

Your aim as an interviewer is to get the person talking. The worst kind of interviewee is the taciturn person who answers in monosyllables.

Do you like London?

Yes.

Are you planning another series of *Kiddytime*?

No.

This kind of interview can make you feel desperate. How are you going to establish a rapport if you can't even get a conversation going? At worst, you could end up with nothing to write. No-one can guarantee a responsive interviewee, but open-ended questions help to square the odds in your favour. An open-ended question is a question which can't be answered with a simple "yes or no". So, instead of the above, you would rephrase the questions to encourage a detailed response:

Why do you like London?

What plans are there for another series of *Kiddytime*?

To write open-ended questions, begin your questions with Who? What? When? How? Where? Why? To illustrate the point, here are some questions I might have asked and received a monosyllabic reply. Alongside, the same open-ended questions.

Questions that invite a yes/no answer	*Open-ended questions*
1. Was it hard to get into television?	How did you break into television?
2. Do you enjoy your job?	What do you enjoy about your job?
3 Your colleagues describe you as an "achiever". Are you?	Why do your colleagues describe you as an achiever?
4 Do funny things ever happen on the show?	Can you tell me about one or two funny things that have happened on the show?
5. Do you think you will become typecast as a children's TV presenter?	Some people become typecast as children's presenters. What's your opinion?

The wrong questions

"Who was it, again, you played in Dynasty?" you ask Joan Collins, having landed an exclusive interview with the star. Don't be surprised if she throws an Alexis Colby-style tantrum. The interviewee will judge you by your questions and if they appear stupid, so will you. So don't show off your lack of research and don't ask negative, apologetic questions either:

> "I wonder if you would be prepared to talk about . . .?"
> "I don't suppose you could tell me more about . . ."

Instead, phrase the questions positively and ask directly.

> Tell me about . . .?
> Tell me more about . . .?

Don't ask questions which reflect your own prejudices. If you do this, you're writing the interview before you leave home. A journalist sent to talk to a 41-year-old actress once asked the following series of questions:

> Is there a paucity of parts for middle-aged actresses in Britain?
> Was turning 40 a crisis for you?
> What do you think about HRT?
> And what about cosmetic surgery? Would you consider it?

The writer was me and I still blush to think about it. The questions revealed my own preoccupation with age – suitable for a piece entitled "Facing up to 40" but not for a general profile.

Multiple questions (many questions in one) are also very confusing. The person won't know what you're talking about. Or she'll answer only the first question.

> Considering what you've written about the importance of the family, would you say a woman's place is with her

family at home? Or would you say it all depends on the woman?

Don't ask questions the interviewee can't understand. If you are talking to a child, or a foreigner with poor command of the English language, you will need to phrase your questions in simpler terms. In general, avoid technical jargon except when talking to experts. Watch out for clumsy phrasing and vague questions:

What do you think of women TV producers?

Another category of questions to avoid is those which stray off the subject matter. With every question you ask, the other person will ask himself: Why does he want to know this? So if you veer wildly off the subject matter, you are certain to arouse suspicion and even hostility. It's particularly important to exercise caution in matters of privacy and personal background.

A leading question is one that suggests the answer by the way in which it is phrased:

How often do you beat your wife?
Do you feel upset when your Dad ignores you?

You should be very wary about leading questions which literally "put words in people's mouths". A politician will know how to handle this, a child or a person unused to interviews is at your mercy.

Questions that get results

You have three main aims with your questions. 1. Get the interviewee talking. 2. Encourage her to give you anecdotes and examples so that your profile is full of interesting and colourful stories. 3. Find out something about that person no-one else knows. Below are a few of the areas you could explore.

Grievances

Everybody enjoys a good moan. A particular bugbear passion-
ately argued can form the basis of a good piece. So give your
subject the chance to be negative and to get it all off his chest.
Ask:

> What do you hate about your job?
> Is there any part of your appearance you dislike?
> What is the trait you most deplore in yourself?
> What is the trait you most deplore in others?
> What depresses you?

Questions to get the person talking

> Has there been a formative experience in your life?
> What's the single biggest risk you've ever taken?
> What's the most important thing you've learnt in your life?
> Has there been a big turning point in your life?
> What's the single biggest decision/choice you've ever had
> to make?

Questions about childhood

> What were you like as a child?
> Tell me about your brothers and sisters.
> What did your parents do?
> Which single person has had the biggest influence on you?

Questions about ambitions

> What unfulfilled ambitions do you have?
> What would you like to have been if you weren't a boxer/
> actress/writer?
> They say success is motivated by one of four desires: de-
> sire for love, desire for money, desire for recognition or
> desire for power. Which applies to you and why?

Questions about what makes them happy

> When and where were you happiest?
> When last did you cry?

Questions about beliefs

> Do you believe in God?
> What would your motto be?
> You're 50 years old. What do you know for sure?
> (Apparently, this is one of Oprah Winfrey's favourite
> questions and it certainly sounds good to me.)

Questions about the human side

> What's your greatest weakness?
> What's your worst habit? (People love hearing that rich
> and famous people wear the same socks for three days.)
> Who's your best friend and why?
> Have you ever felt suicidal?
> What are your vices?

Top tips from professionals

What professional journalists say about interviewing experts

> Often I'm faced with a topic I know nothing about. Instead
> of preparing a list of ready-made questions, I let the experts
> do the thinking for me. I'll say: "For an article such as
> this, what are the most important issues to cover?" Then I
> ask "What's controversial about this?" This unleashes a
> whole hotbed of things that leads to an interesting article.
>
> Joyce Walter, health writer

Don't be afraid of looking silly. Experts live in a world of their own which to the ordinary person is utterly confusing. If you can't understand what they're saying, ask them to "break this down for a five-year-old". If you can't understand it, how can you pass the information on to your readers? In general, experts love explaining things to you – they're flattered.

Val Sampson, journalist

What experienced interviewers say about writing down your questions

I prepare about ten to 12 questions which I try to memorize. That way the interview goes much more like a conversation. At the end I'll say: "I think we've covered everything – let me just check." I don't refer to it as a "list of questions".

Val Sampson

I type my questions out and staple them to the hard inside of my reporter's notebook. I highlight a key word of the question. So if the question is: "Do you believe in God?", I'll highlight the word *God*. I keep my finger in the notebook and can easily flick back to my questions if I lose the thread.

Anne Lloyd, journalist

The importance of the warm-up

Never go in with something controversial. Start from the obvious, get the basic information you need and then move on to more challenging questions. Try to win their confidence with some easy questions, then open it up.

Joyce Walter

I ask two or three easy questions to get the ball rolling, something they'll like. "What's the film you most enjoyed?", "What made you want to do the part?" It's quite a good idea to get the publicity stuff over with first. The new book they want to promote, the new play they're in.

Anne Lloyd

The value of research

If it's a person who's often been interviewed, you don't want to repeat everyone else's questions. So I do lots and lots of research. If the celebrity has an agent, I'll ask for background information and have a general chat: "What does he like talking about? What does he not like talking about? Is there anyone who knows him with whom I could have a telephone conversation?" I'll get newspaper cuttings from the library. When I've gathered all my research, I'll sit down and focus in. I look for what strikes me about that person and his work. In short, I try to find a way into that person no-one else can.

Anne Lloyd

I'll see the play he's in, watch the film, read the book he's written. And I won't just skim it either. I read all the cuttings. Hidden somewhere in the last sentence of a two paragraph piece you might find out that the person hopes to adopt a child. You could pursue that in the interview. What you are after is something new.

Val Sampson

Sell your interview again

What is the difference between the beginner and the professional? The beginner sells her interview once, cashes her cheque and then forgets all about it. The professional writer gains as much mileage as possible out of one interview.

Would you drive all the way to an out-of-town hardware store and then buy only one packet of nails? No, it would be a waste of time. But think of all the work that you did on the interview: right through from suggesting the idea to the editor to preparing your questions, to carrying out the interview and writing it up. Are you going to waste all that work by selling to only one market?

Being a successful writer is as much about salesmanship as stringing words together. If you like, think of the material gained from the interview as a product. No-one else gained exactly the same anecdotes from the subject. You have a unique product to sell and you should sell it as widely as possible. Another good reason to sell your interview again? If you're serious about one day making a living from writing, you must learn to maximise your earnings. Even if writing remains a hobby, you may as well reap the best reward.

So let's take an example and see how the beginner and professional would handle it. A famous actress has agreed to give you an interview – a general interview for *Best* magazine. Great. The beginner begins to prepare his list of questions.

The professional asks: "I've landed an interview with Actress B. What other potential selling opportunities are there? Who else might be interested in this person? What other markets can I think of?"

As a general rule, it would be over-ambitious to expect to write two general profiles out of one interview unless the markets and angles are very different. But the market abounds with sharply angled pieces. *My Speciality* (what the person enjoys cooking), *A Room Of My Own*, *My Latest Discovery* are some current examples. You can also consider fillers, short news pieces that would fit into a magazine as a piece of showbiz gossip. If you are going to interview several famous people, you could slip in one question "What are you hoping to get for Christmas?" Ask several people who are well known and you have the basis of a very saleable round-up.

Let's say you are interviewing a local entrepreneur who has recently set up a juggling company. Think before you go about your questions and you could sell material gathered to a journal for entrepreneurs, a sports magazine, a national and a local newspaper.

Once you've decided which magazines you'll go for, you need to think carefully what each editor will want answered in order to satisfy his readers. The time to ask those questions is now. Think how annoyed you'll be if you think of the perfect market for a piece after the interview but forgot to ask the pertinent questions!

Checking your questions

Two heads are better than one. If I'm going to interview a well-known person, I'll ask a friend if there's anything he'd like to know about that person. Writing is a lonely business and it's easy to get caught up in your own interests and preoccupations. You might have missed out something vital and obvious. So before you set off to do the interview, check your questions against this list:

1. Have I thought up two or three easy questions to get the ball rolling? (They don't have to appear on your list but will help to give you confidence.)

2. Have I asked every important question related to my angle?

3. Have I satisfied the requirements of all the markets where I intend to sell this interview?

4. (When interviewing well-known people) Have I asked the obvious questions that would occur to every writer or have I tried to "find a way into that person that no one else can"?

5. Do my questions lead on in a reasonably logical sequence or dart wildly from subject to subject? (I write down my questions as they occur to me, then try to arrange them in a sensible order.)

6. Have I thought up enough questions? (The only predictable part of an interview is that it will be unpredictable. I can't think of anything worse than running out of questions. Don't expect to be able to make them up on the spot either. While

some people talk at length on each and every subject, others will rattle through your agenda.)

7. Are all my questions open-ended?

8. Do my questions reflect my interests or the interests of the readers?

9. Would any of my questions cause offence?

10. Have I marked the priority questions? (If you run short of time, you may never get to the questions at the bottom of your list.)

7

THE BIG DAY

So the great day has arrived. You've confirmed the appointment and your bag is packed. You've got your notebook, spare batteries, spare pencils, a copy of the publication and a stomach full of butterflies. Don't panic. If you follow the professionals, step by step, you'll feel considerably easier. Start by opening the interview. You need to:

- introduce yourself
- set the person at his ease
- establish the purpose and parameters of the interview
- establish rapport and trust

Opening the interview

There's a saying (used in a TV commercial for dandruff shampoo!), that you never get a second chance to make a first impression. How true. From the moment you appear on the doorstep and open your mouth, the interviewee will be forming an impression of you. Those first few minutes are make or break. So smile your best smile – however nervous you may be feeling, shake the person's hand and say: "Hallo, I'm (your name) doing the interview for (name of publication)."

One of the commonest fears of the new writer is that the interviewee won't take him seriously, "What if she finds out that I've never been published before? I can't really say I'm a journalist, can I, when I'm still working full-time at the record shop?"

Relax. Everyone has to start somewhere. The interviewee is far more concerned about what you are going to ask her. If you're confident and use the professional techniques outlined here, there is no reason for the interviewee to be suspicious.

Don't forget you are not the only one feeling nervous. The personnel director of the sausage factory is concerned to represent his company accurately. The expert on breast cancer is anxious to put his controversial points across fairly. The jovial comedian knows you'll find him sterner/older/fatter than he looks on TV.

Both of you need to relax. If you're at a house or office, it's usual that the person will offer you some refreshment and while the coffee is brewing, this is the ideal time to make small talk. "No, I had no trouble finding parking, thank you." If you jump straight into serious interview questions, the interviewee may feel startled and threatened. Spend too long on small talk, on the other hand, and it'll make her even more nervous. With experience, you'll gauge the right moment to get down to business.

Weeks may have gone by since you made the appointment, so you should open by repeating the purpose of the meeting. "Remember, we're doing the 'My Kind of Day interview' for *Radio Times*." Establishing the purpose of the interview is useful for two reasons: it draws the interviewee back out of her busy life. It helps both of you to concentrate. I usually take a copy of the publication and show the interviewee where the piece is likely to appear and what it might look like.

You should then give the person an idea how long the interview will take and what areas you're likely to cover. "I think we'll need about 45 minutes. I'll start by asking you about your background, how you got into showbiz, then we'll ask you about your typical day, starting at breakfast and moving on through the day." Ask the person if she has any questions: "Is there anything you'd like to ask me about the interview? Is there anything particular you think we should cover here?"

If the person has any fears, apprehensions or suggestions, deal with them now. Otherwise, she may be harbouring them all through the session. Anything that inhibits the free flow of conversation is potentially damaging. People often ask when the interview is going to be published in the magazine. Answer honestly. If you don't know, say "I don't know but I'll keep you posted". Then you're ready to attack with your first few warm-up questions.

Body language

Another name for body language is "non-verbal communication" or "silent language". These are the unconscious signals we give out with our body of what we are really thinking and feeling. If you want to be a good interviewer, be aware of your body language and that of the other person. For the purposes of the interview, your own silent signals must

- encourage the person to keep talking
- not distract him
- not discourage him from talking

From the moment the interview begins, the other person will be looking to you for direction. So you'll control the interview with your silent language: with the way you sit, position your head, direct your eyes, and grunt or murmur interest.

Start by sitting in the right position – not directly opposite, it's too aggressive. Keep your interviewee relaxed by aligning your body at a 45 degree angle to him. If you are sitting back, relaxed and easy in your chair, diagonally opposite the person, the other person will feel much more comfortable.

Sit in an open way that shows you're prepared to listen. Don't sit hunched up with your arms folded; the interviewee will probably do the same. Show interest by tilting your head to one side, leaning forward, perhaps placing one hand on your chin.

Eye contact is another way to show you're interested. If you look back at your interviewee and you're clearly paying attention, your interviewee will be encouraged to be helpful. If you look down at your list of questions, or nervously across at your tape recorder, they will get the feeling you're bored and may dry up. (So if you need to check your watch or observe details of the room, try to do it when the interviewee isn't looking.) Whatever the subject says, try not to overreact. If he says something with which you violently disagree, don't frown.

Are you one of those people who, when nervous or bored, tends to have a nervous tick: clicking and unclicking the end of your biro, tapping your leg, constantly flicking back a heavy fringe? For goodness sake, sit still. Otherwise, the person will get so irritated it may put him off.

Controlling your body language is far easier said than done. We all have little habits of which we tend not to be aware. For example, when I am concentrating and listening intently to what someone is saying, I tend to frown and look desperately serious. So whenever I'm paying attention, I make a conscious effort to smile from time to time to reassure the other person.

Try a journalism class where pupils take turns interviewing each other and the rest of the class observes you. Get yourself videoed – the best way to reveal bad habits. Your knowledge of body language will also help you understand the interviewee. Is he bored, irritated, sincere or, when accompanied by his answers, even telling you the truth? When your subject suddenly touches his ear lobe, he may be lying. When his head is down, his arms are folded and his legs are crossed, he could be feeling defensive. I discovered all this in Georges Patounas' book *Silent Language* (Allied Training International Ltd, 1986).

Interview etiquette

Remember the salesman who called to see you and left muddy footprints all over your carpet? You'll never gain rapport with an interviewee if you antagonise him. So mind your manners. There is no greater liberty allowed the stranger than to enter someone's abode.

Don't step inside the door or enter any room until invited. Wait until you are invited to sit down and wait until the other person is seated first. Don't smoke (unless invited), chew gum, and touch objects in the subject's office or home. Be considerate if it's raining and your feet are muddy, or your umbrella is dripping. It may work for Detective Columbo to sit down in a grubby raincoat and drop cigar ash all over the carpet, but it won't pay off for you.

Once you get talking, should you use first names? Ask first. And don't use the person's name in every single sentence. Although some people believe this increases empathy, my opinion is that over-familiarity, especially in Britain, can have the reverse effect.

In general, behave courteously. If you are offered a cup of coffee, don't forget to thank the person afterwards. If you want to use the loo or explore the garden, ask. Thank the person warmly for the interview – who knows when you might want to talk again?

Two last words on good manners. When you're warming up the interviewee or, indeed, at any time during the interview, watch your remarks. Avoid personal remarks – "That's a nice skirt you're wearing" – and references to politics, religion, sex or race. Don't ask personal or impertinent questions which meander wildly from the subject area of the interview. A very experienced colleague told me, "I never ask anything about a person's private life that I wouldn't be prepared to answer myself."

What to wear

Your aim as an interviewer is to gain trust and make the other person feel comfortable. Traumatised Mrs Jones of Somewheresville may hesitate to tell her tragic story to threatening, power-shouldered, fashionable you. But she may spill all to a woman journalist in a simple blouse and skirt or a pleasant man in a quiet suit.

I once read that a gentleman is well dressed when "you can't remember what he was wearing". The same rule could well apply to the interviewer. Dress to be "invisible" and avoid distractions. So women should steer clear of jangling bracelets, huge earrings, too great a show of leg or bosom.

A good tip is to match your dress discreetly to that of the interviewee. It is no good doing an exposé of life in a cardboard box if you're dressed in a Savile Row suit. Dress should also be appropriate to the setting. Suit and tie for a man is fine if you're in an office, but hardly suitable if the person's going to show you round the farm by tractor.

I've often wondered how Alan Whicker manages to ask such direct questions, sometimes even downright rude, without being punched on the nose. Is it perhaps because he's always dressed like a perfect gentleman?

Getting the best out of the interviewee

To be a good interviewer, you need to be a good listener. If this isn't obvious now, it soon will be after your first two or three interviews. Let's imagine, for example, you have just spoken to Joan Collins. You taped every word diligently and you look forward to writing a brilliant profile. But – horror of horrors – when you play back the tape, the main voice speaking is yours. Poor Ms Collins tried to answer your questions a number of times but in you jumped, snatching the words right out of her mouth, voicing your own opinions, finishing her sentences for her.

Nothing is so damning as the evidence – the tape when you get it home. If yours is the main voice you hear, you've failed. If you finish off the thought, even if the other person agrees, the phrasing will be yours, not hers. Many people talk too much when they are nervous. If this applies to you, learn to bite your tongue.

Listen and never stop listening. During the interview itself, most people tend to put on their formal "interview" face. But when the tape recorder is switched off, the notebook put away, there is a tendency to breathe a huge sigh of relief. I once spoke to a company director for an hour about a new government grant to invest in his employees. As soon as I turned my recorder off, he visibly relaxed and confessed: "Actually, I think the whole scheme is a load of rubbish".

As well as listening, the novice interviewer needs to know when to stay silent. Silence is a powerful weapon which can be used in two ways: to let the other person talk or to force him to talk. It's only common sense that the less time you're talking, the more time is filled with the voice of the interviewee. (A good general rule is to speak for no more than ten to 15 per cent of the time.)

Another good reason for silence is that, like you, the interviewee may be a little nervous. If he's a nervous talker, you can use this to your advantage. Keep listening, encouraging, egging him on. There is a saying: "Give a person enough rope and he'll hang himself". In interviewing, give a person enough air space and he'll reveal all sorts.

Sometimes, although you have prepared a careful list of questions, you run into the model interviewee. This person is logical, articulate, often an expert in a given field. Without the need for you to prompt, she'll tell the story as it happened, moving chronologically from one point to the next. Don't interrupt her flow by insisting on your script.

There are two more occasions where you should shut up and be patient. Don't forget people need time to consider their answers. The first answer is not necessarily the best – often they'll pause to elaborate. In a human interest interview (see Chapter 3), the interviewee may need time to collect her emotions and continue.

If you ask a question on a particular subject and the answer is unsatisfactory, the best response is to say nothing. If you want more information or a different kind of information, solicit it by staying silent. Silence is a void and people feel an overwhelming need to fill it. If a person has finished speaking and you don't play the game by picking up your end of the conversation, after only the slightest pause that person will automatically start to elaborate.

Professional writers are constantly seeking "anecdotes" – entertaining little incidents which help to flesh out the point. If the person mentions something of interest, insist on specific examples. The company director interviewed in the example above also told me: "We believe people are our company's best asset. If someone is giving of his best, we'll do what we can to develop him."

I asked for examples. "We had one woman who was incredibly timid," he said. "Everybody used to push her around, her husband, her kids, everybody. So we paid for her to go on an assertiveness course."

Be a good listener; know when to be silent; and ask for anecdotes. Master these three techniques and your interview tapes will deliver the goods, not disappoint.

Don't forget the details

In the following profile which appeared in the *Sunday Telegraph*, Judi Bevan has observed minute details of physical appearance to reveal the character, Christopher Davidge, behind the façade.

> Although there have been three generations of Davidges at Christies, there is no chance of mistaking him for an old Etonian. The trouser creases of his double-breasted suit are a little too sharp, his black loafers too highly polished, the bracelet of his Cartier watch is just a touch too shiny and his swept back hair too immaculate. This is a man who left grammar school with two O'levels, trained as an estate agent and graduated to selling menswear in Petticoat Lane at 20. (© Judi Bevan, the *Sunday Telegraph*, 1993)

Don't expect your tape recorder to do all the work. Be like Agatha Christie's Poirot and gather all the evidence before you jump to conclusions. You have five senses at your disposal – touch, smell, taste, sight, hearing. Use your sense of touch to feel the firmness of a handshake, the springy pile of expensive carpet. Sniff out the predominant aroma of the person – Miss Dior, cigars or oil paint? A food writer lets you sample her pie – how does it taste?

Look around you – discreetly. Is this a person who wants to impress or a person relaxed with his image? Is the decor austere or fussy, tidy or a mess, light and spacious or dark and enclosed? What sort of books are on the bookshelf? What unusual mementoes? Who is in the photographs? In a dressing-room full of cards, who has signed them?

Like Poirot, you should always be looking for the details that don't add up. Lunching with six-feet tall comedian, Robbie Coltrane, Jan Moir in *New Woman* magazine noted that the strapping Glaswegian ordered a Diet Coke, joking "Don't tell the lads".

The observant interviewer also loves distractions. How does the person behave when a child enters the room, the telephone rings, his Great Dane bites your leg? If another person is present, how does the interviewee interact with that person?

In an interview with Dustin Hoffman in the *Independent* magazine, Mark Lawson recounts how the press agent laboured to bring the interview to a close.

> "You're trying to stop this?" asked Hoffman. "I gotta finish this story . . ."
> "I'm not doing anything, Mr Hoffman," said the Head of World Publicity.
> (More conversation by Hoffman)
> The Head of World Publicity slipped a piece of paper on to my note pad: "Just get up and walk out," it said.
> "Leave him! I gotta finish this point!" growled Hoffman.

In the above interview, Dustin Hoffman "bounced to his feet". How does your interviewee move about? Is she quick or slow, graceful or clumsy? Is her walk jaunty or subdued? Any unusual mannerisms?

There's a last sense – hearing. If your tape recorder's done its job, you'll be able to listen at your leisure for nuances and speech patterns. But use your eyes now to see *how* an answer is made. Has your interviewee spoken for effect or is she sincere? Details, details, details. If you want to produce a great interview, you can't afford to miss a trick.

Controlling the interview

Once when chat show hostess Oprah Winfrey interviewed Elizabeth Taylor, TV viewers witnessed an interview disaster. Ms Taylor was sullen and uncooperative. Ms Winfrey was desperate. "Speak to us, Elizabeth, please, then we can all go home," she pleaded on camera. Watching chat shows gives you a good idea of the sort of things that go wrong.

The first rule to remember is that it is the interviewer who controls the interview, not the interviewee. You have three aspects to control: the other person, the subject matter and the time.

Controlling the other person will be the most difficult part. Will she be monosyllabic or suffer from verbal diarrhoea? Will he be open and spontaneous or so guarded you come away with nothing? The path to getting the story is strewn with obstacles – which is why the next chapter is devoted to tricky interview situations.

For the moment, let's concentrate on subject matter and time. Your questions will map out the subject matter. Take control and you'll feel in control. Reassure your interviewee as the driver of the coach would reassure the tourists, "We'll spend an hour at the Guggenheim Museum, a quarter of an hour in Central Park, then return here to take photos". In the interview you might say, "Let's start by talking about the background – how you became a chef in the first place, then we'll go through a typical day at the restaurant, returning to more specific questions later on".

No decent interview runs exactly to script. I keep my questions handy to remind me what I MUST cover but once a rapport is established, the subject leads on to my questions naturally. Beware the temptation to rattle through your questions as if they were a shopping list. Rather than covering as wide an area as possible, find a fruitful patch and dig deep. The skill is allowing the interviewee enough time to explore the subject and yield interesting anecdotes. Stop the person mid-story and he will be grumpy. But don't let him ramble on either.

The time to draw the subject gently back into the interview is when the answers are boring, completely irrelevant to the subject in hand and wasting valuable time. Then you say, "That's fascinating and I'd love to talk some more about it. But getting back to what my readers need to know . . ."

I believe it is only business-like to give an interview a set time limit. If more than one interview is being attempted, you'll have to divide up your time proportionately. You will also need to ask your questions in order of priority in case you run out of time.

Keep a discreet eye on your watch – but don't keep looking at it or the subject will assume you are bored. Let's say you are doing the kind of interview where you ask a famous personality about a typical day. Don't spend three quarters of the interview discussing what they do from waking up to elevenses, then cram lunch, afternoon and evening into the last five minutes. Pace your questions.

Closing the interview

In theory, the interview is over when the person you are interviewing has answered all your questions. This could take anything from a few minutes – for a simple fact-finding exercise, to an hour or more. In practice, most people have a finite attention span. In my experience, many interviewees show some signs of restlessness after 45 minutes.

You will not need to be a genius in body language to see the signs. She starts tapping her foot, she fidgets with her pencil, looks around or looks at her watch. She might even ask, "Are we going to be much longer? Is there anything more you need to know?"

Some people don't attempt to hide their irritation and boredom. They start to give monosyllabic or even flippant answers. An otherwise friendly, polite person starts to be strained and short. Another sign is that the answers you are getting are not interesting you any longer. It's time to draw the interview to a close. But whatever you do, don't terminate abruptly. Every interview has an emotional structure. During the interview, if you and the subject have established quite a rapport, the interviewee will feel cheated if you snap your notebook shut and exit. In a human interest interview, where the subject has literally unburdened herself and run the gamut of emotions, she needs time to return gently to the present.

If you have planned your questions carefully and kept an idea on the clock, you will find the subject's slight restlessness should coincide with your wish to end. Indicate that you are drawing to a close by giving your words a ring of finality: "Just one more question before I let you go: how would you like to be remembered?". This is a good time to ask about future plans.

If someone were interviewing you, could you be certain to get every fact correct? Could you remember exactly what year you started your current job, how much you were paid, what year you made a film? Where possible, try to check the facts with the interviewee there and then. If necessary, ask him who else might be able to help you.

Keep the doors open. "May I contact you again in case any of my notes are unclear?" If the magazine needs photos, or is sending a photographer, this is the time to discuss pictures (see Chapter 10).

As you get up to leave, thank the subject warmly and reassure him again that he has been helpful: Say : "You've given me some really excellent material. I've got stacks of information here. Thank you so much for talking to me."

Most important of all, keep in touch. As a new writer – and particularly in the area of celebrity interviews – you are in the business of building up what are known as *contacts*. So when your profile is published, send the person a copy and a polite letter thanking him for the interview. Keep in touch with him from time to time and find out what he is doing. The material you have gathered today will be excellent background for future pieces. File it.

8

TRICKY INTERVIEW SITUATIONS

An interview is not unlike a driving test. However well you have prepared yourself, it can all go horribly wrong on the day. Let's look at some of the commonest problems experienced by new (and not so new) writers. Some of your troubles may even start before the big day.

Typical problems and their solutions

Q. What do I do? Interview the person and write the article on spec or first get a definite commission from the magazine?

As a beginner with no prior reputation, you are trapped in a Catch 22. The magazine is unlikely to commission you when they don't know the quality of your writing. You will be submitting the article on spec. But you can't write a word until you've done the interview. So you'll take a risk. But you should limit that risk as much as possible. First make sure the magazine is interested in your idea and that the person you propose to interview is suitable for the publication. Then if you decide to go ahead, be honest with your interviewee. If you haven't got a commission, tell them the truth. Say "I propose to offer this piece to *Woman's Journal*".

Never simply go ahead with an interview on a hunch that "that would make an interesting piece for somebody". The vagueness of your idea may mean you forget to ask the right questions for the publication. It can also be embarrassing afterwards to have spent an hour in someone's company and then not find a buyer for the article.

Q. The person wants to be paid for the interview. What do I say?

Say no. As a freelance writer, you can't afford to pay people for talking to you. Indeed, it is far more reasonable that they should pay you for talking to them. Many writers make excellent livings in the world of public relations penning articles about companies who seek more publicity.

When asked "What about payment?", famous celebrity interviewer Andrew Duncan has a neat answer. "I get paid very nicely, thank you." I agree with him. It simply isn't ethical that a star should be paid for an interview. Without writers like you, how would they have become famous in the first place?

What about human interest interviews? Sensational headlines have led Josephine Public into believing she can make a fortune by selling her story to the media. But in truth the publication is very unlikely to come up with the thousands she has in mind. That is not unless her story is truly sensational and two or three magazines are in competition for it. Don't commit yourself until you have spoken to the commissioning editor of the magazine and ask her what she would be prepared to offer, if anything.

Q. Who pays for coffee/lunch/the taxi home?

The first celebrity I ever interviewed was an actor, in a pub and I'm embarrassed to say that he paid for the drinks. This goes against my advice to you that the interviewer picks up the tab. Where a woman is interviewing a man, old-fashioned chivalry (or friendship as above) may prevail but the interviewer should always offer to pay.

For many reasons – not least the need for sophisticated recording equipment – I avoid interviewing over lunch. Even if the magazine is paying expenses, you may not be reimbursed for two or three months.

Take control and suggest only places where you know you can afford a pot of tea or round of drinks. If you do end up paying more than you'd bargained for, make the writing good and consider it an investment in your future career. Speculate to accumulate!

Q. What if they change their mind about being interviewed?

Writer Duncan Fallowell once drove to the South of France to talk, as arranged, to Graham Greene only to discover that the author wasn't "in the mood" that day. If this happens to you, you'll have to use all your powers of persuasion to appeal to the person's better nature. Remind them they agreed to the interview and you have a job to do. They will usually come round. In the case of the reluctant human interest interviewee, a gentle approach (see Chapter 3) can work wonders. Never forget that the person is often a great deal more nervous than you. Try to discuss their fears. Most people will feel a moral obligation to talk to you once you're there in person.

Q. I haven't seen the film the celebrity is in. Should I pretend?

Trust is essential in an interview. And if you're telling lies, why should the other person trust you? What are you going to do if, having pretended you've seen the film, the actor asks for your comments? While you should make every effort to have done your research – particularly if this is the hook for the article – be honest. If for some reason, you've been unable to do your homework, say "I was able to get video X but not Y. But I particularly enjoyed video Z."

Q. I couldn't help feeling the person I was interviewing was
   lying to me. How should I handle this?

If quizzing an expert for facts, or talking to Joe Bloggs for a human interest feature, trust your judgment. If you have doubts about what you're hearing, check with alternative sources. If necessary, drop the story.

Famous people are in the business of promoting a certain image and will, on occasion, give you a doctored version of the truth.

One American actor told a colleague of mine that he was 28 and single; it later transpired that he was 37 and married with kids! I had the eery impression that one famous person I interviewed was simply making up his life, i.e. telling me what he'd like it to be, not what it was. Your only option with this kind of person is to set down the truth as he tells you and let the reader draw his own conclusions.

Q. Help! I'm afraid I won't get the interview done in the time.

If you have planned your list of questions, you will have taken the precaution of asking the essential questions first. For a profile based around the launch of a new book or film, it makes sense to get the plug over with at the beginning. After that, don't panic. It is much more important to hit the right button and get the person talking on a subject which really interests than to plod robotically through your questions.

Would more time help? Journalist Lynn Barber once spent five days with Keith Floyd, stranded on a remote Orkney island, but found her article about him was "not noticeably richer as a result". I feel a time restraint is good discipline and sharpens the senses.

Q. I get so worried about what to ask next, I can't listen to what the person is actually saying.

When I play back tapes, I often find I've asked the same question twice even though the other person has already replied. The hardest part about interviewing is the need to divide your brain into at least four compartments. One part is listening fascinated to what is being said; another part is picking on an interesting point and resolving to return to it; yet another is thinking what to ask next; the fourth is mentally writing the finished article. Try not to get so caught up in this juggling act that you stop *listening*. Use your list of questions as a reminder so you can *listen* to what is being said. Jot down points you want to return to. Practice makes perfect.

Q. What happens if I take an instant dislike to the person I'm interviewing?

I'd advise new writers to pick people they think they'll like and are interested in. But as a professional, you should be able to talk to anybody. However obnoxious or provocative the person is being, beware of getting involved in an argument. The confrontational interviewer so often seen on TV appears to get results but his target is captive and in front of an audience, yours can get up and leave the room. Arguing achieves nothing and merely fills the tape with your voice, not theirs.

You could view this problem as an opportunity. Many journalists see the "difficult" interviewee as a challenge. Notoriously difficult types make better copy. The tension between the two of you can provide an electricity you won't get talking to "nice" people.

It could be, in a human interest interview, that you are talking to a person who has done something despicable, perhaps selling drugs. You can't be expected to like the person but you must for the time being suspend your disapproval. Keep even any disapproving thoughts out of your head as some people believe the other person can sense what you are thinking. Imagine you are a scientist doing the first interview with a Martian.

Q. What do I do if the person I'm interviewing tries to interview me?

This is a sign that the person is interested in someone other than herself and can help to break up the tension of the monologue. It could also be that the person is curious about some aspect of the interview and it's better to address her concerns now rather than allow her attention to wander. But time when you're talking, is time wasted. The sooner you can get back to asking the questions, the better.

Q. What do I do if I'm just getting monosyllabic answers?

There are several reasons this may be happening. In the case of a famous person, it could be that he is undergoing the interview under duress – perhaps unwillingly sent by his publicist. Depending on your personality, you could handle this in two ways. Chivvy him into giving you the interview, "Come on, now, I've got my job to do just like you," or engage his interest with gentle flattery and informed comment. A more confident journalist might simply terminate the interview. It is surprising how people pull themselves together when it looks like there may be no interview at all.

Perhaps you're irritating the person with stupid questions which show you haven't done any research, such as "What did you say the title of your last book was?" It's far more likely that you haven't yet touched on a subject that really appeals. Uninspired questions produce uninspired answers. Keep probing.

Some journalists recommend solving the problem of the monosyllabic person by putting quotes into his mouth: "Would you say that such and such is the case?" If the person says yes, then the quotation is what follows. I would regard this as a last resort.

Depending on what kind of piece you are writing, a string of monosyllabic responses could provide you with the theme of your profile – it has been done with great skill and wit in the past.

Q. I can't bring myself to ask this really personal question – it might upset them?

The best way to ask a difficult question is to come straight out with it. A colleague of mine once interviewed three women for a piece on HIV-positive women. She had to ask the horrendous question, "Have you planned your own funeral?" A question like that is difficult enough but harder if you try to postpone it. It may be even trickier to ring the person back later. Human beings are remarkably brave and you'll find that they do not react as adversely as you had feared. One technique is to follow a very hard question with something much softer.

Hard question: Why do you hate your father?
Softer follow-up question: You're awfully fond of children. Why?

Q. The person keeps straying off the point. Help!

If the angle of the feature is the relationship between a father and son, that's what you need to hear about. Not his political views, the state of education, the price of Jaguars. It's time to take control. You've got a job to do. Don't be afraid to interrupt and lead him firmly back to the subject matter of the interview.

Q. I couldn't understand a word the person said. How will I be able to write the interview?

I once spent two frustrating hours trying to interview a civil service manager. She was heading up an ambitious new project and I was to review it in a trade magazine. But the more she explained, the more baffled I became. Then I switched off my tape recorder. Suddenly, the same official was talking English. In two minutes, I'd grasped the entire concept.

There are two lessons here. One is that some people are paranoid about talking to tape recorders and take "being interviewed" very seriously. With such a person, you're a lot better off chatting over a beer and trusting to memory. Second, officials, experts or employees interviewed about their jobs can be defensive and lapse into jargon as a form of protection. If this happens, don't even pretend you can keep up with the technical side, ask them to explain. After all, you're going to have to make it understandable to ordinary readers.

Q. What do I do if I suspect the famous person I'm interviewing has been drinking?

If you have the impression that a person is tired and emotional, it really isn't playing the game to carry on with the interview. Have a discreet word with the agent or publicist and rearrange the appointment. If the character is known to have a predilection for long lunches, make sure your appointment is in the morning.

Q. What if my tape recorder jams?

Or you forget to switch on the mike, to change the tape. This is the interviewer's worst nightmare and happens to everybody eventually. One interviewer I heard of became so engrossed in the conversation, that he kept turning his tape over, unaware he was taping over precious material.

One precaution is to use two tape recorders and to take notes as well. You could ask the person to talk to you again. You could trust to memory and check crucial quotes over the phone. As a general principle, buy the best equipment you can afford – those who earn their livings at celebrity interviewing pay several hundred pounds for a machine. Have it regularly serviced and check it's performing properly on the day of the interview.

Can I see your copy? (No)

It won't be long before someone asks "Will I be able to see what you've written?" There are several good reasons not to show your finished words (known as copy) to interviewees if you can avoid it. The first is practical. How will you meet your deadlines if you have to wait for approval of everyone mentioned in the article? You'd never get any work done.

Allowing people to look at your copy also invites them to make changes. As you become more skilled at bringing people out, your subjects will be surprised at their candour. Their quotable phrases which were spontaneous and sound so great in your write-up may make them shudder when they see them in black and white.

Only saints and the supremely self-assured will be able to resist tinkering with your typescript. I once quizzed the languages consultant of a training company for a feature in a business magazine. (It was the magazine's policy to let people see the copy.) Here's what the consultant actually said to me – the quotation I used at the end of the article:

> "Bloggs & Co. has really put its money where its mouth is."

Here's what she "said" after approving the copy.

> "Bloggs & Co. is increasingly seen as a leader in the development of integrated language and vocational training."

Flows off the tongue, doesn't it? In celebrity interviews, the question of copy approval is particularly tricky. I don't subscribe to the view of one writer who told me, "If you give someone copy approval, they never approve it unless you call them God in every sentence". But I do believe the more manipulation there is behind the scenes, the blander the writing becomes. When Glenys Kinnock published her book *By Faith & Daring – Interviews with Remarkable Women*, (Virago) she allowed all her subjects to see the copy. Journalist Jan Moir, herself no mean interviewer, reviewed the book in the *Guardian*. Her view was that if you approached your subject "with such an attitude of unwavering respect, promised complete copy control and then simply edited down the words, presenting the person's thoughts and dreams in a first person stream of consciousness", then you'd end up with "a great deal of bland, self-indulgent deadwood".

If you are going to allow copy approval, you must ask yourself where journalism stops and public relations starts. Are you a journalist or a mere extension of the person's publicity machine? Is it honest?

"One of the reasons I don't like copy approval," writer Duncan Fallowell told me, "is that it's underhand. A kind of conspiracy between the editor, the writer and the star. It gives the celebrity an absolutely clean bill of health and that's outrageous." The same writer feels "paralysed" and unable to write at all if he knows a celebrity has to approve his copy.

Can I see your copy? (Yes)

So when is copy approval appropriate? One case is when you're writing for a regular slot (My Favourite Holiday, My Speciality,

The House where I Grew up etc.) where a person, usually a celebrity, talks in the first person singular. It is as if the famous person himself wrote the article where in fact, you, the writer, wrote it. When commissioned to do such a piece, you will be working to the editor's instructions but don't always expect the famous person to like it. I submitted one such interview taking great care, as asked, to include as much individual detail as possible. The editor was happy but, when the celebrity was asked to approve the profile, she threw her arms up in horror. She rewrote the interview replacing every interesting fact with something non-committal.

On what other occasions should you show a person what you've written? If it's a very technical subject – perhaps an expert on genetics has explained the complicated arrangement of chromosomes – by all means check with the source to ensure you have the facts right. But there's no need to send them the whole article – for speed, you could read the relevant passages over the phone. This is checking for factual accuracy not copy approval. Experts and editors will be impressed by your professionalism.

Perhaps you're earning money doing a bit of public relations. In this case a company or individual is paying you to write what they want and you've no option but to gain approval. No wonder the quotations on press releases can sound so unnatural!

The subjects of delicate human interest interviews may need to see copy for their own protection. If you decide to show them a draft, make it quite clear that once it leaves you, i.e. arrives at the magazine, you have no more control over it. But don't leave the manuscript with them. Check what you can over the telephone.

Finally, you should always show someone a copy if it's a condition of the interview.

Off the record/on the record

Let's imagine, for a change, you're in the hot seat. A journalist takes you out to lunch and you find yourself revealing all kinds of things you never intended. The second bottle of wine doesn't help and the journalist is such a warm, sympathetic person . . . But suddenly you realise you've said far too much so you plead, "Please consider this off the record".

Off the record means a person will speak to you as an individual but doesn't want the remarks to be published. Can the interviewee trust you? There are many times in interviewing when you'll have to wrestle with your conscience. If you have a juicy hunk of gossip or a gift of a quote, it can be hard to resist using your information. More hardened writers than me will say a person shouldn't talk to journalists at all if the information isn't to be made public. But if you betray such confidences you do so in the knowledge that the person may never talk to you again. As a freelance, can you afford to antagonise your sources and lose your contacts for the future?

Off the record can also mean that you may use the material provided you don't name the source. Some people may risk losing their jobs (or friends!) for expressing certain opinions. If what they have to say is helpful to your research, it is well worth agreeing to the request "Don't quote me on this".

Better safe than sorry

As a teenager in the 60s, I had a job babysitting a little girl during the holidays. One day I was forced to take her with me to a hospital appointment. The nurse assumed I was a teenage, unmarried mother and was curt. But she was making an assumption about my relationship with the child. As a journalist, you're in the business of facts, not assumptions. So make sure first. If you get such details as relationships wrong, you could be sued for libel.

Libel is when you defame somebody's character in writing. The legal criteria are:

- Does the matter complained of tend to lower the person in the estimation of society?
- Does it tend to bring him into hatred, ridicule, contempt, dislike or disesteem with society?
- Does it tend to make him shunned or avoided or cut off from society?

There isn't space here to go into a detailed explanation of the libel laws. Try *McNae's Essential Law for Journalists* by Walter Greenwood and Tom Welsh (Butterworths). It is worth noting that someone you quote in a feature can libel another person in what he says. For example, the manager of a boxer says, "Joe Hardhead is a great boxer but thick as two short planks". If you report his remark, you're also guilty of libel.

National newspapers – in particular, the so-called gutter press, and publications like *Private Eye*, may decide to fly in the face of the law for the sake of a good story. But they have deep pockets. As a freelance you simply can't afford to take the risk. If you are in any doubt about the legal side of a story, ask the publication's lawyers to have a look at it, or consult your own solicitor. Be aware that as a freelance you will be liable and a serious party could potentially sue you and the publisher. Use your common sense and, if in doubt, leave it out.

9

WRITING UP THE INTERVIEW

The interview's over, it went well and you can't wait to get down to the writing. But first there's that little matter of transcribing your tape. Sounds easy, doesn't it? But it's the part about interviewing many journalists loathe.

Transcribing your tape

To transcribe a tape means literally to reproduce in written form everything that was said. There before you, you'll have the raw material from which you'll fashion your feature. Transcribing a tape, at its worst, is like being a dictaphone typist working for a boss who mumbles or speaks far too fast. At best, it is an entertaining and integral part of the writing and editing process.

First get comfortable with your equipment. I use a small Sony tape recorder which is mains-operated and sits on the left hand side of my desk next to my keyboard. If you're sharing a room, it might be more sociable to use a personal stereo and headphones, though constant rewinding will quickly use up batteries. If you're a whizz typist with sensitive feet, you might try an old-fashioned pedal-operated Dictaphone.

Now for the bad news. The reason most writers complain about transcribing is the time it takes – three to four times the original interview. (You should bear this in mind even during the interview and press the pause button if you're merely chatting.) It can be particularly irksome if the person constantly paraphrases, uses technical jargon or talks very fast.

You can't make transcribing less irksome but you can make life easier for yourself in several ways. Take a few notes as well as taping. Not only is this a good insurance policy against the tape jamming, this will give you a map of where the tape is heading. If you believe something particularly interesting was said, use the digital counter to locate the passage on the tape. You can skip the bits you said, and any bits where you were chatting (heaven forbid), you can also skip parts you think you haven't a hope of using. If you're very pushed for time, you may have no other option than to play the tape and pick out what you consider to be the best quotations. But this is far from ideal.

Could you avoid the labour of transcribing your tapes by employing a typist? Some writers do this; others consider it cheating. I tend to agree with a colleague who describes transcribing, rather poetically, as "an integral part of the creative process, like being a painter and stretching your own canvasses". It's true. In the transcribing process you do a lot of editing, conscious and unconscious, while you're mulling over your material.

Use the two or three hours where you are working on your tape as a gestation period for the creativity which is to follow. And, incidentally, there's no better way to improve your interview technique than by listening to yourself.

The different interview formats

The market determines how you'll write up your material. Your profile might appear as: *question and answer* (known as Q & A), *rolling monologue* or in the *narrative form*.

Question and answer

Made popular by American *Playboy*, the question and answer form (Q & A) is less common here. It takes up space, so magazines use it more than newspapers. While some publications stick to the same set of questions each week, in others, it's up to you to draft both questions and replies. The questions appear in one typeface, the answers in another.

Q & A is deceptively easy, so you will be surprised how much editing it takes to get a satisfactory result. For a start, you may need to rephrase questions to put the reader in the picture. In a Q & A for *Best*, I asked one actor from the North of England whether he'd had to change his accent to get work. In the interview I asked "Did your accent ever prove an obstacle to you?" but in writing up the question I gave the readers more information:

> You're from Salford, Lancashire. Did your accent ever prove an obstacle to you?

The rolling monologue

Many regular slots are written in the first person singular as a rolling monologue. This is true for the vast number of celebrity interviews with such names as: True Confessions (a famous person reveals the gaps in his reading for a books supplement).

With an articulate and interesting interviewee, you will practically be able to insert speech marks and let the interview roll. In most cases, quite a bit of editing and rearranging is required.

Don't forget that the A Life in the Day or whatever theme you are writing on is not the point. No reader is desperate to know whether a person has cornflakes for breakfast. They want you to show them the human side. Talking to a work-oriented TV presenter for *Radio Times*, I decided she should reveal a little more of the personal, human side. So leading on from a long paragraph describing a typical morning at work, I inserted two short paragraphs about personal ambition and family background.

> If I weren't a TV presenter, I'd like to be a barrister. It could be something to do with being in front of an audience. My dad was a solicitor and my mum a journalist.

> I'd like to go round the world at some stage. Everybody says you should do it after university, but I didn't and once you get on to the career path there's never a right time.

I could not have included that information unless I had gathered it at the interview. Even if the theme doesn't seem to demand it, always ask about background.

In the rolling monologue, it is as if the famous person himself is speaking even though you, the writer, wrote it. So be careful to retain original speech patterns. Let's say the person is Irish, don't lose the lyrical rhythm of the intonation. Don't use the word *kids* if the person would naturally say *children*.

The narrative form

Finally, we come to the narrative form, the form you associate with written interviews. From the writer's point of view, this is the biggest challenge and the greatest opportunity for creativity. Unlike regular slots where the theme is implicit, it will be up to you to bring the person to life and to structure the piece. But first you have to arrange your material.

Tips on writing the profile

Before you can write a word, you need to organise your notes. Whatever system you come up with, make it easy and workable. As some wise person said, research is only as good as your retrieval of it.

After a long interview, the transcript alone can be daunting, running to several pages. One way to break this up on the page is to use three differently coloured highlighter pens. You might use one colour for background, one for useful information, a third for direct quotations. Another method I have heard of is to divide your transcript into three categories: A material which must be used; B material which is desirable but not essential; and C material which is expendable.

While transcribing, you will have already started to mull over your material and a theme should begin to emerge. You may be tempted to look for the most startling quotation and begin with that. But write the profile up without using any quotations and see how far you get. If you're merely stringing out a block of text with quotations, this will soon become apparent. Writing without quotes makes you determine what you're talking about.

When will you quote directly, placing the remark inside speech marks, and when will you paraphrase, i.e. reflect the gist of what is said? A good rule is to quote a subject only for effect, not for routine information that can be expressed more succinctly. For example, you would not use quotes to convey mundane fact:

"My first movie was called *Blood on the Water*."

but you would if the quote adds impact to the feature:

"*Blood on the Water* made my blood boil!"

Never start with the chronological details. *Jack Superstar was born on a quiet estate on the outskirts of Durham*. You will have to include background somewhere but put it off as long as possible and then introduce at a point where it is justified. Don't panic if that point is 1800 words into a 3000-word piece.

As usual, the way to find inspiration is to read other people's profiles. Start with Sunday magazines and upmarket monthly publications such as *GQ*, *Vanity Fair* and *Elle*. Interview styles are subject to fashion like everything else. For an overview from 1859 to the present day, read *The Penguin Book of Interviews* edited by Christopher Silvester (Viking). In *Mostly Men* (also Viking), journalist Lynn Barber demonstrates in 33 encounters why she finds the temperamental characters most appealing. In some profiles, the character of the interviewer, rather than the quarry, seems ever-present. Read *A Little Light Friction* (Futura Publications) – a book of 49 interviews – by Val Hennessy and decide whether you think this is intrusive.

Openings with impact

Could you resist the following introduction to a profile by Val Hennessy which appeared in *Time Out*?

> Sitting on Martin Amis's lavatory I gazed down on his bidet full of books and back copies of the *TLS* and marvelled at the strange ways of the upper-classes who obviously keep their books in their bidets in much the same manner as the working-classes keep coal in their baths. To tell the truth I was playing for time sitting there on Amis's lavatory. Taking deep breaths, dropping a Valium, running my hands under the cold tap, I was trying to cool out and curb an overwhelming urge to rush into the next room and smash the beady-eyed Amis in the face. (© Val Hennesy)

This opening not only takes place in an unexpected setting, it contains a forceful reaction to the other person. Could you take a tip from film directors and open your interview in an unusual location? You're unlikely, as a new writer, to be as candid as Ms Hennessy above. But it's still good to start with the your first impression. However much a person has been interviewed, he's never been interviewed by *you*. Does he look like a male model only skinnier than you expected? If her screen persona is intimidating, did you find her more approachable in the flesh?

Another good way to open is with an anecdote. A story the person tells about himself or, more commonly, what others have told you about him. This can sum up the theme of the profile. Quizzing Judge Pickles for the *Independent on Sunday*, Lynn Barber used her research to provide the basis for a tantalising opening.

> Let me kill any suspense right away: he didn't grope me.

Having hooked the reader, she then expanded on the background which led her to expect such behaviour. (I read this interview from start to finish and not because I was interested in Judge Pickles.) Where the profile has a strong topical hook, you may need to open by reminding the reader why the person is in the limelight right now, particularly if your subject is only temporarily famous or has been out of the public gaze for a while.

Yet another great way to open is the knock-em-dead quotation. But in the narrative form profile, you can't rely on stitching together great quotations. Find a strong theme and use your opening to put it across. In the following interview with comedian Billy Connolly in the *Telegraph Magazine*, author Mick Brown does just that:

> He was once the uncrowned king of Glasgow, but Billy Connolly no longer maintains a residence in the city. "I don't feel that connected to Glasgow any more," he confesses. The hotel where he is staying in the West End of the City – quiet, discreet, expensive – is only two miles, but a lifetime, away from the working-class tenements of Partick where he grew up. (© Mick Brown, *Telegraph Magazine*)

Endings that satisfy

Master chefs take care to dream up spectacular desserts. Why? Because this is what lingers in the diner's mind, long after the meal is over and leaves a lasting impression. Never let your writing meal peter out without a grand finish. There are numerous ways to leave the reader uplifted and satisfied.

One of the most popular ways to end an article is to refer to the opening. The writing proceeds in a kind of circle and ends back where it started. It has a satisfying rounded-off effect. For example, interviewing actress Diana Rigg for the *Telegraph Magazine*, writer Stephen Pile opens:

> Enough is enough. Nowadays Diana Rigg will be interviewed only by men. Henceforth, women journalists will not be allowed past the gate because they ask searching personal questions.

He concludes:

> . . . she had not minded this interview as much as some others because I had asked her about her career. "The questions were worth answering." I glowed briefly. Exit a male reporter. (© Stephen Pile, *Telegraph Magazine*)

There are many ways you'll find you can refer back, e.g. picking up on an anecdote, turn of expression, a person's physical appearance or manner. I once wrote an article suggesting readers save money on hair and beauty by visiting London's beauty schools. "If you're going to job interviews, even if you're short of money, you must keep appearances up," was the message of the introduction. I closed with : "Best of luck with that job interview."

Another good way to end the interview is with a reference to future plans, particularly if it is not what the reader expects. What plans do you have for the future, I asked an actor known for serious roles.

> I've always wanted to do a musical. I don't think, that, even in my mid-40s, it's too late to have a crack.

In the same way that the quotation is an excellent way to open a piece, it's a fine ending, too. Some writers even have an unwritten rule: best quotation to open the article, second best quotation to close it. Whether you obey this rule depends on how confident you are the reader will get to the ending.

In the previous section, I suggested that the opening can sum up the whole theme of the piece of writing. So can the ending. In the following piece on Dame Catherine Cookson in the *Sunday Telegraph*, writer Jane Shilling allows the author to sum herself up.

> "Tom [her husband] always says, 'It's not a bit of good, she'll have the last word,'" says Catherine Cookson. "So I'll have that on my tombstone: She had the last word."
> © Jane Shilling, the *Sunday Telegraph*

Polish, polish, polish

If an editor asks for 1000 words, 1000 words is all she wants. While you're checking the finished piece for length, check also for length of sentence, paragraph and number of quotations usually used by the publications. It's good style to keep your sentences no longer than about 25 words with the motto: one thought, one sentence.

It's far easier to cut a piece of writing than make it longer. If you're convinced that all your material is wonderful and you can't possibly cut, give it to a friend. Select a person as close as possible to the target reader and ask her if there was any part of the content she found less interesting than the rest.

Once I've finished the piece of writing, my next step – time allowing – is to put it away for a couple of days, overnight at the very least and rest the copy. That way, when you pick it up again, you've gained some distance from the material and can read it as a reader not writer. Another good tip is to read your material out aloud. This way, groanworthy phrasing becomes immediately apparent.

You may not ever aspire to be a sub-editor (those mortals who will check your work for accuracy and grammar), but a course in subbing (sub-editing) is an excellent investment. It keeps you in touch with what is currently considered good style and can lighten your writing. After one such course, I resolved to change *whilst* to *while*, *however* to *but*, and to make sparing use of the words *special* and *very* (often redundant). Another good tip is to remove all mentions of *nearly*, *approximately*, *almost* and not to juxtapose similar sounding words e.g. *fairly*, *shortly*.

A cliché is a hackneyed phrase made trite by overuse. For example, she looked as beautiful as a princess in her wedding-gown. Of course, you wouldn't use such a tired expression but, when in a hurry, it's easy to put down the first phrase that springs to mind. Yes, *springs to mind* is a cliché, too.

Another instinctive check I will make is that I've used the active not passive voice. For example, it is better to say *Paul took me to see the movie* than *I was taken to see the movie by Paul*.

As soon as possible, often at the query letter stage, I will give my work a title. Many writer's guides tell you titles are not important, the assumption being that the publication will change your title anyway. I disagree. For a beginner writer, submitting on spec, the catchier you can make your heading the better. Follow the style of the market, and if they use two word titles, so should you. Alliteration works well as in *Shocking Sara, The Determination of Diana, Danson Delivers* (three examples picked at random out of my files).

The manuscript's as good as you can make it. Before sending it off, run a final check for grammar, spelling and punctuation. A sure sign of the inability to punctuate is the misuse of *its*. *It's raining today* but *the cat lost its collar*. You may think it's unimportant but editors won't.

10

ANY OTHER BUSINESS?

You can double your chances of a sale by offering pictures. It is easier to sell average quality words with average quality pictures *as a package* than an excellent photograph or superb article *on its own*.

The selling power of pictures

Sit yourself in the editor's chair and imagine you've received a great interview. Your next step is to lay out the page and make it look attractive. The picture editor(s) – or you, if it's a small magazine – will now have to scout around for an appropriate illustration or photograph. Had the writer sent you good quality pictures, your job would be done. Pictures increase your chances of a sale because you can offer editors a package – words and pictures. The first article I ever had published was a travel article about Turkey. Not only did the editor agree to buy my words, she used one of my pictures on the front cover. I collected two separate fees. You don't have to be a professional photographer to sell your pictures, nor do you need elaborate equipment. I use a fully automatic Nikon compact camera where flash, focus, rewind and zoom are all built in.

Know what editors are looking for. Forget the colour prints you snap on holiday. Newspapers, and any publications printing in black and white, will need good quality 10" x 8" prints. Colour magazines need 35 mm colour transparencies (trannies) or slides. So you'll need to buy slide film (e.g. Fujichrome rather than

Fujicolor). Don't forget to caption your slides and mark them with your address.

When taking photos, the most useful tip I've ever heard was

P - people
I - involvement
C - composition
S - symbol

Readers are more interested in *people* than things. So if you're writing about a cook, don't show us a close-up of the cake, but the cook with his cake. Now get the hero of your picture *involved*. He'll look more interesting icing the cake than posing awkwardly, hands by his sides, in front of it.

Next look at the *composition*. Never have the subject bang in the middle of the frame, looking at the camera. Place him to one side. What about framing him in the kitchen doorway or encircled by hanging pots and pans?

A *symbol* supports the activity described. Let's say you've interviewed a family with 14 children. You could simply photograph them but they'd look more interesting sitting around the enormous saucepan they use for morning porridge or with the stack of bread they eat in a week.

If you can't take your own pictures, let the editor know where pictures are available. TV channels and other press offices – needing to promote their programmes – will let you have colour transparencies of celebrities FREE. Offer pictures but don't send them yet in case they go astray.

As a general rule, the smaller (and therefore poorer) the magazine and the more unusual and remotely situated your interviewee, the more grateful magazines will be for pictures.

What rights have you sold?

Sooner or later you will hear about author's rights. There are serial rights and there is copyright. Neither is as complicated as it sounds.

If submitting to a magazine or paper, it is normally assumed that you have sold first British serial rights (F.B.S.R.) unless otherwise agreed. Some writers mark their manuscripts (and invoices) F.B.S.R. in the top right-hand corner.

If you were then to sell the manuscript in the United States, you would be selling first North American serial rights.

You can sell *the identical set of words* again to another British market provided you tell them it has already been published in this country. That way you are selling *second* British serial rights. Let's say you've sold first British serial rights of a celebrity profile to *TV Quick*, you could then offer *second* serial rights to your local paper or monthly magazine e.g. *Cheshire Life*. Selling second rights is not financially exciting but gives you the advantage of another by-line (your name under the article) in a new market. You'll get to know another features editor and expand your network of contacts.

Magazines often ask to buy *all rights*. With celebrity interviews, in particular, sell them *F.B.S.R. only*, if you can. That way you, not the publisher, will make money by selling the interview again in other countries. If you can't negotiate this and have to sell all your rights, be sure you do so for a fat fee.

Copyright is different again. As soon as you put your idea down in writing or take a photograph, you own the copyright and are protected against having it stolen. Usually, this right applies for the length of your life and 70 years thereafter. Although you can copyright the way your idea is expressed (the words), you can't copyright an idea. It is possible that two writers can come up with the same idea at the same time. Bad luck if someone else gets there first.

Money, money, money

Compared with the thrill of getting into print, money can seem a secondary consideration to the new writer. You won't work for nothing, of course, (see my comments about this in chapter 2), but you're not yet in a position to haggle over fees. If, in due course, you decide to earn your living from your pen, your attitude will change. You'll expect to be compensated for the effort spent researching and writing your articles, and you'll watch the post eagerly for signs of a cheque. You'll notice some publications are slower to pay than others.

Most magazines pay on publication, not acceptance. Of those which pay on publication, the best of all are the newspapers which usually send out cheques at the end of the following month. Many magazines take up to three months to despatch your money and one or two may never pay you.

To help prevent the latter gloomy situation, there are a number of measures you can take:

- confirm the fee and the commission in writing
- be cautious about working for tiny, newly established magazines. Never do a second article until you've been paid for the first
- make sure you know what the payment is and submit your invoice *on the day you deliver the article*

Two other points worth noting are that: you may be able to claim expenses such as travel to the interview but check first; if your article was not used but was commissioned, you will be entitled to a *kill* fee, sometimes all, usually less, of the original fee. By the time one magazine decided to run an article I had sold them, *a year later*, it was worthless. The businessman I had interviewed had gone bust. I received the full fee.

Even if you're not at this stage earning much from your writing, it is business-like to record your expenses. If you make a profit (earn more from your writing than you are spending on deductible expenses), you will be liable to pay tax.

Getting down to work

If this were a book about how to write novels, your next task would be sitting down to write. With articles for magazines, you have to sell your *ideas* first. The procedure is:

- research markets and jot down ideas in an ideas book
- select *one or more ideas* for a *specific* market and do enough research on them to write your query letter(s)
- send your idea(s) off to the editor

If you are still not sending off ideas, perhaps you are too ambitious. You fancy writing about "men who won't commit" for a women's magazine, but you'd also like to interview celebrities, pen crime fiction and devise TV sitcoms. It's a common problem among creative people to have leanings in many directions but if you want to succeed, get focused.

Objectives should be simple, achievable and measurable. Example, a week from today I shall have sent idea X off to *Ice Hockey World* magazine. The moment that query letter vanishes into the post box, you've taken a positive step towards launching yourself as a writer.

Is your problem that you do finish the query letter but you never send it off? Perhaps you're too much of a perfectionist. You could prepare query letters in a formal environment such as an adult education class in journalism. That way you'll have a tutor and colleagues on whom to test your ideas.

Once the editor says yes, he'd like to see the full article, you should ask for a deadline. If he doesn't give you a date, make your own. Professional writers – threatened with the sack or starvation – have to write but most of us wouldn't take our dressing gowns off without a deadline.

Your support network

If you want a successful writing career, invest in people. As vital to a writer as paper, other people are:

- consumers
- comrades
- contacts

Many writers are extremely secretive and protective about their work but if your article is going to be read in a magazine, it's worth trying it out on a real life reader. Other people (writers or not) are consumers. When you're starting out, why not meet informally with two or three like-minded friends every fortnight and simply read each other's articles and query letters?

The comrades you'll meet in a writers' group will provide invaluable support through the long, lonely days of rejections. Find such groups in *The Writers' and Artists' Yearbook*, *The Writer's Handbook* or ask in your local library. Judge a group by the success of its members.

In London, I belong to a professional women writers' network consisting of some 300 people (Women Writers Network, 23 Prospect Road, London NW2 2JU). Among the members, I can instantly find interviewees and anecdotes for almost any subject I am writing about. I can swap tips and pick up leads of which editor is looking for what.

New writers talk about meeting people, professionals call it *building up your contacts*. So get out and about, meet editors and other writers in different fields. Avoid making enemies. If you antagonise a celebrity's agent, don't expect him to be friendly next time you want to interview another artist he represents. Staff journalists move from paper to paper and up the ladder. Be friendly to the assistant editor on Magazine X; tomorrow he may be the editor of Y.

Growing your career

It's only common sense to send more ideas to the editor who bought your first piece. Once a magazine has bought several articles and knows you are reliable, the day will come eventually when the editor phones *you* – in other words, your first commission.

It would be unwise to stick to the one or two markets where you've been successful. The magazine could go bust or the editor you like could leave. Instead, give yourself the added confidence that you can succeed in a wide number of markets. Keep your horizons wide until you've decided what you really want to write. Do you see your writing as a career or as an entertaining hobby? Telephone research for articles can be tricky from a full-time job. If you decide you'd like to become a freelance, whatever you do, don't pack in your day job until you're sure you can survive. Many talented contributors to prestigious publications still finance the food in their fridges by other less glamorous writing work. Perhaps they edit company newsletters, medical journals or write advertising brochures. One success in the *Guardian* does not a guaranteed annual income make. You'll need some regular means of income until you find your feet.

And finally . . .

Over the last 109 pages, I've written many words on how to write and sell interviews. But the art of interviewing could be summed up in one word:

LISTEN

Good luck and may your tape recorder keep on rollin'.

APPENDIX

Your address
Date

Ms Josephine Bloggs
Health Editor
The National Newspaper
Address

Dear Josephine Bloggs

If it's true that a third of those in work believe their employment is theatened, (Gallup survey for the *Daily Telegraph*, Date), then those employed are experiencing more stress than ever.

SUGGESTED 350 WORD PIECE – JUGGLE YOUR TROUBLES AWAY

The ancient art of juggling is enjoying a revival – as a new form of stress relief.

Worlds away from the circus, accountants at Dun & Bradstreet are learning how to juggle to relieve pressure of work. A Cardiff G.P. prescribes juggling for stress relief and a Norfolk man is convinced that learning to juggle has helped to alleviate pain from his latent stomach ulcer.

Is it true that juggling has a calming effect similar to that of meditation? And why is learning to balance several balls in mid-air supposed to be good exercise for the brain? Can anyone learn?

In the course of this piece, I shall visit a juggling workshop and talk to computer systems analysts, advertising executives and other professionals about their experiences.

ABOUT ME

An advertising copywriter by profession, I have written for *TV Quick*, *Best*, *City Limits* and *Campaign* among others.

If you are interested, may I have an idea of your usual rates?

I look forward to hearing from you.

Best wishes

Fig 1: Example of a query letter

111

copyright Martin Hopeful, month, year

Mervin Megastar – My Kind of Day
by Martin Hopeful
800 words
one reproduction only
first British serial rights

Martin Hopeful
12 Optimist's Lane
Getrichquick
GT3 4SH
Date
Tel. No.

Fig 2: Sample cover page

APPENDIX

(800 words on 4 pages)

Martin Hopeful
12 Optimist's Lane
Getrichquick
GT3 4SH

Tel No.

MERVIN MEGASTAR – MY KIND OF DAY
by
MARTIN HOPEFUL

Your first paragraph should be arranged flush left, thereafter you indent all subsequent paragraphs by five spaces.

So the next paragraph starts here.

Fig 3: How to lay out the first page of your article

Your address
Date

Ms Josephine Bloggs
Megastar Management
Celebrity House
Fame Street
London

Dear Josephine Bloggs

I refer to our telephone conversation regarding Ryan Rockstar and have pleasure in sending you more details.

This is to confirm that *Woman's Magazine Y* would be very interested in talking to Mr. Rockstar for its monthly, whole page feature entitled "Ladies in My Life". This would involve $^3/_4$ hour talking to a journalist who would then write the piece.

I know how concerned stars are to protect their privacy and their loved ones and would like to reassure Mr. Rockstar that this column need not intrude into family life. "Ladies In My Life" is a broad brief open to creative interpretation and the feature could touch on such areas as female friends, mentors, attitudes and influences, the qualities he admires or appreciates in women musicians, whether women are more musical than men etc, etc.

Past interviewees include: U, V, W, X, Y and Z (list of impressive-sounding famous people who've been featured in the column). I am sending you some cuttings to give you an idea of the wide potential of the subject matter.

Deadline to get into the March issue (on sale 14th Feb) is mid-November, for an April issue (on sale 21st March), mid-December. We would certainly run a para under the interview promoting Mr Rockstar's new TV series as and when you have details.

Finally, I understand how difficult it must be trying to reconcile all the demands for Mr Rockstar's time. I can do the interview anywhere, anytime to suit. Trust you will do your best for us.

Best wishes

Signature

Name

Fig 4: The written approach

INDEX

Accuracy, importance of, 19, 32, 34, 91, 102

Agent(s), 3, 41-2, 47, 66, 78, 88, 109

Alzheimer's Disease Society, 47

Amis, Martin, 99

Anecdote(s), 5-7, 59, 62, 67, 76, 77, 79, 99

Anonymity, 26

Aspel, Michael, 16-17

Action on Smoking and Health (ASH), 7, 46

Angle(s), 17, 38, 48, 57, 87

Appointment, interview, 53

Approach
  celebrities, 41-2
  editors, 15-18, 28-9, 114
  press officers, 38-9
  human interest interviewees, 26-7

Barber, Lynn, 98-9

Batteries (tape recorder), 54, 70, 94

Beatty, Warren, 58

Beginners'
  mistakes, 33
  markets, 10-11, 23-4, 39-41

Bella, 4, 7, 23, 25, 31, 33

Best, 4, 5, 27, 43, 67, 96

Bevan, Judi, 77

Body language, 50, 72-3, 80

Breaking in, journalism, 1, 11, 24, 37, 44-5

British Film Institute Library and Information Service, the, 48

British Safety Council, 7

British Associations, Directory of (DBA), 46

Brown, Mick, 100

Calendar, journalist's, 15

Career, growing your, 109-10

Case history (ies), 5, 21

Catch 22, 37, 82

Celebrity,
  definition, 35-6
  interviews, 1, 18, 20, 35-45, 81, 90, 96
  human interest feature, 22
  round-up(s), 18, 40-1
  slots, 39

Celebrities
  approach, 41-2
  research, 47-8

Channel Tunnel, 7

— Safety Authority, 7

Cheshire Life, 40, 106

Choice, 13

City Limits, 44

Clippings, 18-19, 47, 66, 81

Collins Joan, 61, 75

Coltrane, Robbie, 77

Commission, 37, 40, 43-4, 53, 82, 107, 109

Competition, from other writers, 11, 14, 19-20

Composite (type of feature), 5

Composition, picture, 105

Computers, 20

Confidence, 3, 18, 29, 39, 41-2, 52, 56, 68, 110

Connolly, Billy ,100

Contacts, 1, 41, 81, 92, 106, 109

Control, interview, 78-80, 83

Cook, William, 44-5, 51

Cookson Catherine, 101

Copy, approval, 89-91

Copyright, see Rights

Close, interview, 80-81

Cuttings, see Clippings

Dates and Events, Encyclopedia of, 14

Daily Mail, 12

Daily Telegraph, 4

Dates, Dictionary of, 15

Debate(s), 5, 14

Dee, Jack, 44

Details, importance of, 31-3, 72, 77-8, 91

Difficulties
  with interviewees, 85-8
  with questions, 87

Dislike/disapproval, of interviewee, 85-6

Distractions, 72-3, 78

Dobson, Lesley, 33

Dogs Today, 40

Dress, suitable for interview, 74-5

Duncan, Andrew, 83

Edit, write-up, 96, 102

Editor(s), 13, 15-18, 29, 33-4, 43, 59, 91, 103, 104, 108-10

Elle, 37, 98

EMAP Women's Group Magazines, 10

Endings, write-up, 100-1

Etiquette, interview, 73-4

Eurotunnel, 7

Evening Standard, 39

115

Expenses, 25, 83, 107
Experts,
   how to find, 46-7, 88, 91
   talk to, 2, 3, 5, 7, 8, 49, 51, 64-5, 84
Eye contact, 72

Fallowell, Duncan, 84, 90
Femail, 4
Fillers, 67
Files, 18-19
Fire Brigades Union, 7
Fonda, Jane, 37
For Him, 45
Former Film Stars, 37
Foundation for the Study of Infant
   Deaths, 26
Freedom Organisation for the Right to
   Enjoy Smoking Tobacco (FOREST), 46

Glitter, Gary, 44
Goals, realistic, 36
Greene, Graham, 84
Guardian, the, 4, 44, 90, 110
GQ, 37, 98

Hennessy Val, 98-9
Here's Health, 39
Hoffman, Dustin, 78
Hollis, Press & Public Relations Annual,
   47
Hook
   timely, 14-15
   topical, 13-14, 17, 38, 41, 43, 59, 99
Hopkins, Anthony, 4
Hostility, 62, 85-6
Human interest features/interviews, 1-2,
   8, 20, 21-34, 50, 58, 76, 80
   market for, 22
Humphries, Barry, 44

Ice Hockey World, 108
Ideas, 4, 8-9, 24-6, 28, 108
Independent, the, 14
   magazine, 78, 99
Independent Television Commission
   Library, 48
Infant Deaths, Foundation for the Study
   of, 26
Interview
   close, 80-1
   control, 78-80
   equipment, 54-5

etiquette, 73-4
open , 70-2
prepare for, 46-55
sell again, see Repeat sales
telephone, 50-2
types, 7, 4
write up, 94-103
Interviewee, get the best out of, 75-7
   types, 7-8
   find, 46-7

Jackson Michael, 37
Jam, tape recorder, 55, 88-9, 95
Just Seventeen, 10

Kill fees, 107
Kinnock Glenys, 90

Lawson, Mark, 78
Lay out/presentation, 20, 112, 113
Libel, 92-3
Lies, lying
   you, 43
   interviewee, 84-5
Listen, ability to, importance of, 2-3, 75,
   85, 110
Location, interview, see Appointment
Looks, 10
Lumley, Joanna, 18

MacLaine, Shirley, 44, 58
Magazine(s),1, 4, 8-13, 15, 22, 35-6, 58,
   67, 83, 95, 98, 105, 107-10
   payment by, 107
Manchester Evening News, 47
Manners, see Etiquette
Market(s), 12, 18, 67, 68, 108, 109-10
   beginners', 23, 39-40
   for your work, 9-10, 22
McDonalds, 8, 46
Middlestars, 37
Mizz, 57
Megastars, 37
Moir, Jan, 77, 90
Money
   for you, 20, 106-7, 110
   for interviewee, 83
Ms London, 9, 13
Multiple questions, 61-2

Narrative form, (interview format), 95,
   97-9

National Union of Journalists (NUJ), 11
Nerves/panic/fears,
   you, 29, 51-2, 56, 70-3, 75
   interviewee, 56, 71, 76, 84
News of the World, Sunday magazine, 40-1
Newspapers, 1, 4, 9-14, 18, 22, 25, 35-6,
   93
   payment by, 107
   pictures, 104
   source for ideas, 25
New Woman magazine, 77
Non-smokers' Rights, Association for, 46
Notebook, 70
Notes,
   take, 48-9, 88
   unclear, 81
   organise, 97

O50, 10
Objections, to interview, 26
Official organisations, 47
Off the record, 91-2
Oldtimer Showbiz Greats, 37
On the record, 91-2
Open-ended questions, 59-60
Openings, write-up, 98-100, 101
Open, interview, 70-2

Patounas, Georges, 73
Payment, see Money
Persuasion, powers of, 2, 27, 84
Photocall, 42
Pictures, 9, 55, 81, 104-5
Pile, Stephen, 100
Polish, write-up, 101-3
Publicist(s), 42, 48, 86, 88
Publicity, machine, 38-9, 90
Planning
   your calendar, 15,
   submissions, 38
Playboy, 95
Plug, 38-9, 42, 85
Prejudices, 61
Preliminary conversation, 27, 50
Prepare, interview 46-55
Presentation, 19-20, 112, 113
Press officers, 42, 46-7, 50
Problems, interview, 82-9
Professionalism, importance of, 19-20,
   71, 109
Profile, 4, 14, 59
   how to write, 97-8

Query letter(s), 15-19, 108, 109, 111
Question and answer, (interview format),
   95-6
Questions
   check, 68-9
   essential, 58-9
   leading, 62
   open-ended, 59-60, 69
   prepare, 56-69
   run out, 68-9
   that get results, 62-4
   wrong, 61-2
Quinlan's Illustrated Directory of Film
   Stars, 48
Quotations, 5-7, 32, 91-2, 95, 97-8, 101

Radio Times, 71, 96
Ramble, interviewee, 79, 87-8
Rapport, 3, 45, 54, 59, 70, 79, 80
Real life stories, see Human interest
   features
Rejections, 29, 109
Remmington, Dee, 33, 34
Repeat sales, 66-7, 106
Research, 5, 45,48-9, 66, 84
   celebrities, 47-8
Rigg, Diana, 100
Rights, which sold, 36, 105-6
Rising Stars, 37-8
Rolling monologue, (interview format),
   95-7
Roddick, Anita, 58
Ronnies, The Two, 48
Ross Diana, 37
Round-up(s) 4,7, 40-1, 50, 51, 67
   celebrity, 18, 40-1
Royal, human interest feature, 22

Scotsman, the, 44
Screen International Film & Television
   Yearbook, 48
Sell, overseas, 10
   pictures,104-5
   rights, 36, 105-6
   to editors, 9-10
   interview again, 66-8, 106
Shilling, Jane, 101
Shorthand, 49
Silence
   fill, 30
   importance of, 75-6
Slant, fresh, 14, 17

Slot (s),
   regular, 4, 39, 67, 96
   celebrity, 39
Small talk, 71
Smile,
   at interview, 70
   on telephone, 52
Smouldering, issues, 26
Social Services, Department of, 47
Social Services Year Book, 47
Southern Life, 40
Specialise, 39, 44-5
Spotlight, 41
Style
   right for human interest features, 31
   good, 101-3
Sub-editors, 57, 102
Suchet, David, 43
Support group(s), 26, 47
Sunday Mirror, 23
Sunday Telegraph, 77, 101
Sunday Times, 14, 37
   — magazine, 58
Sundries, 37
Sylvester Christopher, 98

Taciturn/monosyllabic, interviewees, 59,
   78-80, 86, 87
Take A Break, 47
Tape, transcribe, 94-5
Tape recorder, 49, 54, 72, 77, 78, 88, 94,
   110
Tax,
   deductible, 13
   liability, 107
Taylor, Elizabeth, 37, 78
Telegraph, Daily, 4
   — magazine, 100
Telephone, interview, 40, 50-2
   manners, 2, 51-2
   research, 110
   techniques, 51-2
Third party,
   trust, 26
   set up interview through, 29, 51

Time,
   interview, see Appointment
   run out of, 85
   waste, 79
Timely hook, 14
Timing, of submissions, 38
Time Out, 98
Titles, 102
Topical hook, 13, 17, 38, 41, 43, 59, 99
Transcribe, tape, 94-5, 97
Tricky, interview, see Problems
Triumph-over-tragedy, stories, 2, 4, 21,
   28
True-life dramas, 22, see also Human
   interest features
Trust, 26, 45, 70, 84, 91
TV,
   channels, 38
   magazines, 13, 39, 43
   Soap Stars, 37
TV Quick, 39, 106
Types, interview, 4-5, 95-7

Vanity Fair, 98
Vegetarian Living, 40

Wear, interview, see Dress
What to write about, 8-9, see also Ideas
Whicker, Alan, 75
Whom, to talk to, 7-8
Who's Who, 48
Winfrey, Oprah, 78
Woman, 33
Woman's Journal, 57, 82
Woman's Own, 33
Woman's Realm, 9, 27, 43
Work, get down to, 107-8
Writers' and Artists' Yearbook, 92, 109
Writers' groups/networks, 109
Writer's Handbook, The, 47, 92, 109
Write up, interview, 94-103